MAPPERTON MOMENTS

1987-1995

JOHN MONTAGU

SKYSCRAPER PUBLICATIONS

MAPPERTON MOMENTS
Published by Skyscraper Publications Limited
20 Crab Tree Close, Bloxham, OX15 4SE
www.skyscraperpublications.com

First published 2019

Copyright © 2019 John Montagu

The moral right of John Montagu to be identified as the
author of this work has been asserted in accordance with
the Copyright, Designs and Patent Act, 1988.

Cover concept by Maggi Hambling
Design and typesetting by chandlerbookdesign.com
Mapperton illustration by Barbara Jones

Printed in the United Kingdom by CPI

ISBN: 978-1-911072-39-3

Introduction

I wrote this diary as a means of working out what inheritance means, and the frustration it can involve. It covers the last eight years of my father's life. I had decided in 1986 to give up a desk job with Christian Aid, and I fully admit that I wrote some of the diary out of pique, as a direct reaction to what I was supposed to think or how I was supposed to behave. Writing it out of my mind was also a means of escape from a kind of tyranny. To say that my father had become a focus of discontent would be too simple a conclusion, because I still felt affection for him nurtured in childhood. But there were times of great exasperation which Caroline and I shared when we were trying to help him in his last years, as we had shared them when he was still in control of his life. I do not want him to hold my attention now, any more than I did then. Perhaps someone will attempt to write seriously about him[1], but it would be difficult for anyone who knew him well. In one sense he was the head of a historic family and the life tenant of a country estate. All this gave him a *folie de grandeur* which was part of his sometimes amusing personality.

---

1 See also the mainly political memoir edited by myself and my late cousin, Andrew Best, *Hinch: A Celebration of Viscount Hinchingbrooke MP*, with an introduction by A Lejeune, Mapperton, 1997. I am also grateful to Andrew and his wife Jacky, and to others, for reading this typescript with great care.

But there was, and is, nothing grand about that. The family was no more unusual, or eccentric, than any other. The estate is a residual agricultural property in Dorset which, before he came to live here as a local MP in 1956, had survived death duties, two world wars, continuous sales of land and a lot of extravagant living. My father improved the house and garden, but it was at the expense of the estate and the investments. He brought character to the role, but he was, as politician as well as landowner, unable to turn it around.

This diary provides a few glimpses into the efforts of a new generation to become reconciled to the reality of inheritance – to the maintenance of buildings, gardens and heirlooms, and to the care of individuals involved. My father may have been the excuse for keeping a record, but the people who emerge from the story belong to it just as much as he did, including those close to me who somehow remain in the background.[2]

I know that I could not have taken on this project without Caroline's love and support, and here I am referring to both family responsibility and day-to-day estate management. I could have, like so many others, run away from it. But Caroline has always had a remarkable attention to detail and administrative ability. In addition to all her knowledge of the Middle East, she knows about plants and trees, buildings and farm tenancies, and above all about people. I dedicate this brief record to her and to the enjoyment which we have both had, not without pain, from living – now for over 40 years – in this unusual environment. Our brochure uses phrases like 'fine manor house' and 'beautiful countryside': maybe, but behind the façade of heritage in remote rural England everyone knows there can be a lot of heartache and even blood-letting.

John Montagu, 2019

---

[2]   See below for a list of some of the main characters.

Mapperton Diary

FAMILY

Victor Montagu, Viscount Hinchingbrooke,
aka 'Hinch' and 'Higgy' (1906-95)

John Montagu, son, aka Earl of Sandwich from 1995

Caroline Montagu, daughter-in-law, John's wife,
aka Countess of Sandwich

- Luke, Orlando (Lando) and Jemima (Mima),
  children of John and Caroline

Sylvia and Perceval Hayman, parents of Caroline

Kate and Nicky Hunloke, Hinch's daughter and son–in–law

- Tilly Hunloke, daughter of Kate

Julia Montagu, daughter of Hinch

- Timothy, son of Julia

Robert Montagu and Marzia Colonna-Montagu, Hinch's
son and daughter-in-law

Elizabeth Montagu (Betts), sister of Hinch

HISTORICAL

Edward, 8th Earl of Sandwich, of Hooke Court, also known as 'Uncle Hinch' (died 1916)

Ethel Dora Labouchere (1860-1955), née Munro, owner of Mapperton from 1919

LOCAL AND ESTATE

George and Bobby Brown, Coltleigh

Martin Cake, handyman

Heather and Mike Caplen, cook/handyman

Shirley and Stan Clark, housekeeper/husband, The Flat

Keith Archer (Shirley's second husband)

Roy Copp, builder

Andrée Dorrington-Ward, estate secretary

Jean and John Hodgins, The Old Rectory

Jimmy and Joe Larcombe, 3 Estate Cottages

Raymond Leaf, builder/carpenter

Michael Montero, head gamekeeper

Patsy Mundy, temporary housekeeper, The Flat

Dick and Alice Powell, forester and caretakers, 2 Estate Cottages

David Puzey, Marsh Farm

Joyce Sponsford, ex-housekeeper, married to Alf, 4 Estate Cottages

Mr and Mrs Suddards, Garden Cottage

Cecil and Fred Tolman, plumbers

Mr Kennedy and Jeff Truscott, gardeners

Ethel and Les Way, Keepers Cottage

Jane and Tony Way, cleaner and builder, 1 Estate Cottages

OTHER FRIENDS AND NEIGHBOURS

Iona and Matt Abraham, Mangerton

Daffodil and Derek Andrewes, Loscombe

Joan Best, Hincknowle, and sister-in-law Alice Dilke

Dr Peter Claydon, Whiteparish, Salisbury

Dione (Lady) Digby, Minterne

Frances Fedden (close friend) and Tristan Eckl (her son)

Edward Green, Melbury Estate, Evershot

Dr Michael Hudson, Beaminster

Mary-Rose and Robin Mangles, near Crewkerne

George Martelli, Wooth Manor

Kay and David Mowlem, Petersfield

Steve Scott, near Sherborne

Nigel and Bun Thimbleby, Wolfeton, Dorchester

MAPPERTON
DIARY

1987–1995

Mapperton

M apperton lies alongside an old Montagu family estate, originally based at Hooke Court and inherited by the 5th Earl of Sandwich. The previous owner of Mapperton House, Ethel Labouchere, was a friend of my grandfather George who used to walk over to Mapperton to see her. But it was my father who bought the house and neighbouring farms in 1956, six years before he left the House of Commons.

One of the best descriptions of Mapperton comes in 'Dorset', by Aubrey de Selincourt, published by Paul Elek in 1947.

"Suddenly on my left, not far from the lane, I saw below me, through the misty air, a flush of pink: it was a cherry orchard in blossom. Then, again to the left, a broad drive opened between an avenue of trees, ending in a wide gravelled court surrounded by ancient barns and stables; and there, behind its gates, was the house. It lies so deep in its hollow amongst the trees that one must be right upon it before one knows it is there. With its yellow-brown stone, great bay windows with innumerable panes, the stone parapet above, the tall twisted chimneys, the creepers and flowering shrubs about its walls, the little church which forms the third side of the square round which it is built, and the enclosing trees, it is very solemn, very quiet, and very beautiful. Except for parts of the roof, where the lovely stone tiles have been replaced by slates, neither the house itself nor the aspect of the country for miles around can have changed at all for centuries; nor the rooks either. No doubt there is nothing wonderful in that; but to me at any rate there is a sort of comfort in it."

Mapperton,
Near Beaminster

1987

Monday 12th January

The weather charts kept by my father for many years show that the cold usually sets in during the second week of January: today seems to prove it. (But tomorrow is worse.) I am on my own this week. Andrée, our estate secretary, rings to say she's coming in the afternoon. Les Way rings from Keepers Cottage to say his pipes have frozen up in the roof. His wife Ethel says their son David's have too, in No 5. Luckily Tolmans have two men in the cellar already so they go and help. Martin, the carpenter, is already up in Orlando's room removing the window. I go up to check all is well and find damp spots on the ceiling again.

Move a few boxes to prepare for Hugh Jaques, the archivist from Dorset Record Office, who arrives at 11 a.m. We talk for over an hour while I show him various locations of family papers: he offers hope that someone may be able to help sort unlisted papers, and that the whole collection will stay together, Victorians and all.

After seeing Andrée in the office I go up to welcome Joyce back from hospital: she's just finished a cup of tea with the Powells. Alf meanwhile is busy making the house warm for her.

Rapid meals with my father are becoming the routine: but I linger with the cheese after he is gone. Where is the warmest place to drink a cup of coffee? Kitchen fairly draughty what with icy larders. Choose library but TV so poor I finally retreat to the office. Try to write letters but record a new answer–phone message instead and feel satisfied. Two men deliver the French drawing which has been on loan, after a freezing journey down.

Tuesday 13th January

This day of calamities starts with a minus 12 degrees reading outside the garden door – but Cecil Tolman says it is minus 18 in the wind, the kind that gets under windows in the top attic.... Yes, suddenly I hear drip drip drip in my father's bedroom and the worst has happened: a burst pipe in the attic cupboard exactly above his bed, making a big pool in the canopy which drips rapidly through his mattress, straight through the library ceiling and into my father's *chaise longue*. What a treble! The plumbers and I tear about with tools and towels respectively, up and downstairs for an hour, before the flood is finally contained. Then I spend much of the day, initially with the help of Patsy the housekeeper, carting wet bedclothes down to the Aga and wiping down floors and walls. The new electric blanket has suffered but should dry out. The tapestry bedstead has been hoisting up on the pulleys in the kitchen, and fires are playing on mattresses. Apart from this Mike and Alf now report bursts as well as Alf, the Chevette radiator has frozen, so have two more house radiators and a cistern....

Wednesday 14th January

Last night the snow finally came, and a few inches are piled up against doors and even windows. Again I had to cancel a visit to Dorchester. My father and I and Patsy drove gingerly down to Beaminster. He wouldn't wear his glasses and I cautioned him on the stretch past Storridge where there used to be a sign which said 'Drive carefully or break your neck' – I wish they had left it up. But he drove quite steadily. We found quite a lot of other shoppers stocking up in case of further snowfalls, with the Mace queue right to the back of the shop. My father was sitting in the car with loud music and the engine running long before I got back to the square. I picked up anti-freeze for the Chevette – too little, as it turned out – and we drove back home, dropping newspapers off. George Brown's pipe by the letterbox was choked with snow. Cutlets and delicious currant mush for lunch. I gather the Powells have joined the frozen-up list.

I spent a lot of time clearing up towels and folding blankets after yesterday's mess. Then at about 4 p.m. I went along the landing to see if the bedroom was dry and heard the familiar sounds of a mountain stream and fountains playing directly overhead. Here we go again.... Felt some panic as it was nearly dark, and rushed up to the attic to find the same pipe has burst further along, and was spraying water from several holes into the floorboards behind the skirting. Very hard to dam or get access. I rushed to get tubs and jammed my finger into towels to stop the holes like the Dutch boy, but found the basins filling up every few minutes, with plenty of water pouring through into the 18th century ceiling of the staircase hall where it must have formed a huge reservoir. Eventually I got the Tolmans up again, thank goodness, and they turned the water off – such a simple turn of the valve, but it has to be the right valve. Meanwhile water had continued to dribble through at several points and was flooding the main staircase. Down went the bowls again and the sodden towels. The drips went on the whole evening, and I increased the orchestra by adding two white *cache-pots*. The gale continued to roar down from the attic. Heather said she couldn't get through the snow, so I made a decent supper of soup, cold meat and Stilton already out, adding hot potatoes.

Thursday 15th January

The snow has stopped but is lying in deep drifts, with the wind howling through cracks day and night. After breakfast I clear the front path quite effectively, with Higgy [the children's name for my father] remarking that the wind would only blow it back again and what I should do was shovel it into the yard with the tractor! He sets out for the papers which I later learn have got stuck halfway from Crewkerne. Meanwhile I start to mop up the hall where the water is still coming in because of yet another leak above the curtain where Lord Montagu of Boughton – the Jacobean head of three families – was hanging until I took him down yesterday (a rare bit of providence this week). This leak was pointed out by the Tolmans who came for the fourth time to turn the water back on. More soaked curtains and carpets are carried out to the kitchen.

A fox is seen trotting across the field beside the unruffled Jacob's sheep, pausing to find out who is watching him (several of us) and then disappearing uphill along the Holeacre hedge. Later I follow his tracks and deer traces in among the sheep tracks, and then climb up to the bungalow site with my skis and traverse down to the old hedged lane below Coltleigh. A lot of exercise and a lot of fun – which I feel I deserved. I walked up to the road and skied very slowly home. My father offered the news that his bathroom had now frozen up. The flood has obviously reached Canute....

Friday 16th January

OK, we've had the library and the staircase hall scenes, now for the drawing room drama. In the usual way I was on leak duty, wandering along the landing listening for drips – which I can now hear whether they are there or not, such is my state of preparedness – and I had just checked my father's bedroom and listened for 'music' in the hall when, unmistakably, boom, down it came again, somewhere between the attic stairs and our bedroom door. Whoever is behind these leaks, they sure know how to spread themselves. Quick as a flash I was off to collect the same old pots and pails that have done duty all this week, not forgetting the old log buckets which once filled are quite immovable. I rushed to ring the Tolmans but they are far too busy: Cecil and Ken, that inestimable duo who alone know the plumbing circuit here, are ankle deep in water at Slape Manor, Netherbury. Mrs Tolman promises Fred in due course; meanwhile a passing Mr Kennedy, about to abandon snow-bound flower beds, is quickly recruited and we both hare up to the attic and crawl around in the eaves. Patsy and Jane run helpfully up and downstairs, emptying fast-filling pots, while the water pours on down through the bedroom floor and the attic stairs into the drawing room ceiling, once again forming a lake which eventually dribbles through in a long line of drips calling for more pots and then a whole row of priceless *cache-pots*. Mr K and I locate the burst pipe, hidden behind a tank out of sight and hissing silently, and complete a superb patched-up job with insulating tape just as Fred comes up the stairs. He gives advice, Fred and Ken – Dorset's 'Red Adairs' – eventually arrive with tales of Slape and I am finally left alone with the drawing room reservoir. It is still dripping when Caroline, Mima and her new friend Bella arrive for the weekend. In between I manage to get down to Geoffrey Tiarks' memorial service – last to arrive and first to slip out before the last hymn. And at last the sun comes out.

Saturday 17th January

But the clouds gather again and the snow refuses to melt. No Mr K. A brave band of guns collects outside the school hall. Patsy's dog Benjy charges into the wood at just the wrong moment – next time he'll get shot. When was it that the water started trickling through the ceiling again? And where did it come from? Better not ask, just get out the floor-cloths and mop it up, it's bound to stop. But it doesn't, it sets out in another long line of drips from the clock to the staircase landing, matched by the faithful pots waiting underneath. And it goes on dripping until C and I stick skewers surgically into it so that it drips faster and we think it's going to drain away but it doesn't. Then it's time for the heaters. The plumbers' extension lead is hijacked, carpets are lifted up on to fireguards, stools, anything to hand, while hot air blows on them ineffectively.

Shooting lunch in the hall, rather cold, and I wish I'd transferred some of the heaters there. Luckily one or two guns bring extra drink. Edward Green, the agent at Melbury, is there and a good turnout of the Mangles family – including one on leave from Moscow who, needless to say, feels warm. Later Mima and Bella prepare a Cresta Run on the slope towards Mythe, and I ski over frosted grass to join them. Charades in the evening, very well acted by the girls and not guessed by us. Surprisingly we get a lot of office work done, too. And the drips play on.

Sunday 18th January

I tiptoe out of the bedroom at about 8.15 a.m. praying for peace and quiet overhead, but not a bit of it. There is a drip on the nose of Bacchus – one of four figures at each corner of the stucco ceiling – and the pots are still singing away so I empty them into my father's loo which has mercifully de-iced itself without a visit from the experts. Not so Luke's, apparently, because yesterday morning, I forgot to mention, Caroline descended slowly on to it only to leap up as if she had been scalded: the bowl was full to the brim with icy water!

The morning was busy, with a visit from Bob Gilbert: Caroline and he spent a long time in the office and kitchen discussing current projects. I join in from time to time, especially during first exchanges on a management plan for the Countryside Commission, nipping upstairs to make sure that I have not been caught out by leaks old and new, or to arrange carpets in front of the heater. Then happily the plumbers return and reassure me that Bacchus' nose and ears will stop dripping because they have found the cause; but unfortunately – yes, another leak has developed somewhere behind the bath in the attic and they will try and turn the water off and then come back and fix it later.

There are still a lot of calls coming in – Les and Ethel are in serious trouble again with a cracked water tank and Heather and

Mike need a new cylinder, so they will need attending to. And by the way, said Ken, why didn't we go and live in a smaller house where we didn't get so much trouble; he would never live in a house like this; why did we?

Why indeed? I mumbled something about having to look after things like a museum, but it wasn't convincing.

Tonight my father decided to return to his old bed from temporary winter quarters in the 'chapel room'. He insists on leaving his new electric blanket turned on all night.

Caroline and the girls on their way to London fail to get up the hill in freezing sleet and ice, so they spend another night and we have more charades. The drips have moved back to the attic stairs, relentlessly.

Tuesday 20th January

It doesn't end there. The Old Rectory is next on the hit list. The central heating seizes up because the oil won't flow through the pipe, and the front bathroom pipes freeze. Oh yes, and did I mention that the main hot water cylinder in the cellar has cracked? This was before the freeze, but it all adds to the excitement – and the bill. The loss adjuster is coming from Bristol on Friday – he should have fun.

The attic stairs got soaked again, but my washing machine/ Aga routine with the bathmats is now quite slick, provided I don't trip over the corners of drying carpets or the line of *cache-pots*. This evening I finally turn off the heaters, lay back the carpets and return the tubs, bins and pots to their rightful owners. I shall be almost sorry to miss them.

There was the small matter of the wet patch in the children's sitting room under the skylight, but that had to do with melting ice in the valley behind it, and so doesn't 'count'.

I am still listening, and will probably hear drips all the way up in the train to London tomorrow.

Wednesday 28th January

Writing, or typing, a diary on a daily basis seems impossible unless one is prepared to walk around with a tape-recorder and speak confidentially out of sight of friends and relations. I have difficulty in remembering anything before today, so this will be a very sporadic record; and selective, too.

I came back to Mapperton on Monday, by car from Devizes where I spent the night with my sister Kate after the school play at Marlborough. I brought the news that the first snowdrops were out in Wiltshire, but Higgy said they were already out in the garden, now that the snow had melted.

There are still bright white streaks across the landscape, mainly under the hedges facing north – though the sun hasn't been seen for days. This morning it blazed down from a deep blue sky and warmed us all for the first time.

The morning was spent in office chores and then walking around with Roy Copp and his painter, peering up at the cracks in the ceiling following the floods. The loss adjuster generously offers to redecorate the whole area affected, and bar the bedroom we have accepted. My father took one look at the library ceiling, yellow with smoke and age, and said he'd rather have it that way. He'll have more to worry about when they reach the bedroom and he will probably have to return to winter quarters. Meals were a bit silent. At lunch I told him Patsy had got a job at Hooke school and had decided to walk there and back – about a mile and a half over the fields twice a day, returning after dark. He got rather worked up about it, understandably impatient that she was still occupying the flat after resigning.

I passed George in his yellow jeep this afternoon as I was posting letters on the main road. The dogs were shifted aside and we drove down to Home Wood. We walked up to the pheasant pen, George explaining that he proposed to move the birds downhill to the ride to make sure they flew at the right angle. We found horse's hoof marks and holes nosed out by badgers. I saw a bright red fungus on a twig pretending to be a spring flower. A young roe buck with a white tail crashed downhill, probably one of several. The stream splashed far below. I walked down to the lower gate and back up to the garden. No sign of Mr Kennedy. I felt he must be pleased there are new tyres on the garden tractor. Jeff, on the other hand, is fuming about them because of the marks they will make on the grass. They are like the two figures in the weather box, rain and shine, summer and winter, an odd sort of team.

Thursday 29th January

I spent most of the day in Dorchester, lunching with Steve Scott in the King's Arms which he says Devenish is converting into a modern complex, much to the disgust of the old faithfuls like him. It seemed we were eating the last roast beef and Yorkshire pud before the revolution. We talked about classic cars at the courtyard fair, much more interesting than the legal stuff about the family. I then visited Hugh at the Record Office who showed me ancient maps of Purbeck and old legal registers down in the vaults, a few inches from where county court prisoners apparently sat waiting for cases on the other side of the wall. Very cold again as I drove home. I went down to Melplash Court to warm up – whisky, and a nice vet from the village who looks after Austrian red deer in quarantine on their way to New Zealand.

Friday 30th January

Another bright sunny day, good for walking, so before breakfast I try to revive my cracked old Cordings 'astronauts' with dubbin. I find six grubby white candles in the boot box – an ex tea chest marked 'Ophir Tea, Mincing Lane' which could do with a polish itself. I've been invited to lunch at Hooke Court – once a family home, now the St Francis School for boys.

After breakfast the phone rings, Andrée arrives and the Shorrocks engineer comes to reset the alarm at Garden Cottage while I try to finish the washing up. My father wanders in, searching for the ash bucket, but Shirley fields him. I spend a good hour doing bills and letters, trying to leave the office before anyone else turns up. The marquee people arrive to quote for the Bridport Round Table ball; Andrée meets them. I put on socks and boots and am halfway through the back door when Public Health arrives about the water supply. I manage to put them off until next week and walk to the Chevette. Hardly am I out of the yard when cars appear from nowhere. One is Mike Caplen, off to collect a trailer of manure from Coombe Down (Louisa Wood later told me he got stuck there with two burst tyres.) Somehow I get away up the hill and park in the hedge beside Coltleigh. Now the day really begins.

My left boot begins to give trouble but let's ignore it. First comes the track along to the Hooke road, warm and full of birdsong. For some reason this reminds me of a memorable walk in Bangladesh, six miles to the clinic at Simulia. I round the wood and turn down to the school, heading for a dull, flat-roofed box opposite the truncated shape of old Hooke Court where Uncle Hinch asked Miss Compton from Mapperton to make up a shooting party, c. 1914. Jack and Kath Barnett lead me into lunch with the boys, one verse of a hymn followed by fish, mushy peas and semolina. Then upstairs to see the marvellous chapel under the roof. A policeman arrives to interview a boy about a train incident – we all think he's come for us. Coffee in the common room under an 1880s photo showing the moat and a mysterious lady. Now the moat is reduced to an iced–up swimming pool and a swamp overrun by boys.

Down the road to the village, left at the church and up to see Mrs Walbridge. On the horizon are the towering masts of the BBC relay station and a rambling farm owned by the Vesteys, who Mrs W says gave £50 for the church roof. She has long memories of farming at Kingcombe and Rampisham: all her family were tenants of Uncle Hinch, whom she calls the 'bachelor Earl'. She used to stay with the gardener at Hooke, whose family used to move into the Court in winter. She remembers Sir Peter Scott, the naturalist, staying there as a small boy, with few clothes on as if to prepare himself for Antarctic wastes. My father remembers he was exempt from clothing rules at West Downs, presumably not for the same reason.

Three o'clock, and the sun is still warm as I climb the hill to Hooke Park.

I start down a ride but soon disappear into thick undergrowth, showing years of Forestry Commission neglect. Across a few fields and I am soon drinking a cup of tea with Pam Fooks. Michael wakes up after an exhausting morning fencing the Mapperton grass keep. Nearly four, and I almost have to run down to Burcombe, over the dickey bridge [before we made the ford] and back up to Coltleigh.

Back home my father has already poured Louisa a glass of sherry before I can offer her tea; she is here to discuss arrangements for the shoot dinner. After she leaves, Anthony Kilroy of Lawrence's arrives to inspect the painting of Anne Boyle which got splashed in the floods; it will need revarnishing. Cold meat again for dinner, followed by the news of Terry Waite's capture in Beirut and Dr Worrall's resignation as South African envoy. Very tired as I record this.

Saturday 31st January

The pheasants rejoice on the last shooting day. There are not many left, but plenty (usually up to two in five) seem to have got away altogether.

Five Christian Aid ladies and one husband – Jack Taylor, the electrician – come round the house and give me helpful tips on coffee mornings. These are the valiant crew who made teas in the stable last summer. They ask searching questions about objects in the church which I can't identify.

After shooting lunch in the school hall – sun streaming through half-drawn curtains – I walk with the guns to the bungalow and then across to Hackthorn Hill. A snipe gets up and George courteously waits for me; another gets up and he doesn't wait. Later a woodcock is framed in a green field in front of me but I am chatting to Tony Valdez Scott and receive dark looks.

Sunday 1st February

Church in Beaminster and to my delight Tim Lewis turns up: Canon Eastman, ex St George's Windsor, preaches on the theme that we the people were the temple and not the building, it being money-changers day. Jim White comes up for garden path levelling – to prevent the garden tractor lurching over the edge. The Abrahams come to lunch. Iona has wonderful stories of the four Munro sisters at Mapperton in the early 1950s with their ear trumpets, the youngest complaining that at 80 she was too old to be asked down to do all their dirty work.

Patsy's radiators go cold; someone has apparently turned off a valve in the yard.

Thursday 5th February

Back from London last night in swirling mists which go on till the weekend. Mapperton becomes like a mountain fastness – sometimes you can't even see the stables. Burst pipes are still trickling away in the yard and under the gravel. Not an ideal day for the Suddards (ex teaching in Windsor, theatricals and Bermuda) to see the Garden Cottage but they seem to like it. We decide to drop the rent rather than re-advertise. My father agrees to sound out the Ways on moving to no 5: part of a long saga.

Saturday 7th February

Clear sunny day as I drive along the A303 to take out Orlando and a friend from Marlborough. Kate and Luke meet us in the Raven at Poulshot for a sandwich lunch. Back to Dorset in time to join Francis Gerard and his daughter Kate: we talk about deer farming, South Africa and computer chess.

Snowdrops are coming out everywhere and even the first crocus on the grass circle. Earlier I had climbed with Roy Copp to look at the garden water supply catchments as far as Hackthorn Hill.

They vary from shallow drains to deep manholes. One which was marked as catching springs for the main drinking supply was choked with weeds which we pull out, turning the water temporarily brown.

Sunday 8th February

Drinks with the Thimblebys at Wolfeton. The drive to it is perilous and the characters straight out of Thelwell cartoons. An impressive range of buildings – as close to Dorchester as Hinchingbrooke is to Huntingdon. Lando is in good form after tonsillitis and nearly two weeks in the San. Planning meeting for the Courtyard Fair goes smoothly.

Monday 9th February

I clear away the breakfast, put on the coffee and get the dining–room ready for the first 'coffee morning to discuss a coffee morning'. Past ten and no one appears. Then I look out of the window and see all three farmers' wives arriving at the front door together. Feeling like the nervous bachelor that I temporarily am, I've forgotten to unlock the dining-room, so scurry round, picking up the tray. We then have a very pleasant hour working out the details of this St Patrick's Day bring-and-buy raffle auction affair with Nescafé thrown in. My father and the plumbers hover outside but mercifully no one disturbs us.

Then we get down to the real talking: how one wife is going into hospital (Elaine Puzey) and another (Peggy Fairall) is having an awful time preparing to leave the farm at short notice as it's to be sold – callously it sounds. At the end Bobby Brown and I start talking about a possible retirement bungalow at Coltleigh. Bobby says a few years ago she'd love to have been housekeeper at Mapperton and 'show us all what to do'. Actually she wouldn't have loved it.

Tuesday 10th February

Today everyone turns up at the same time – there are days like that. Tolmans field a very big team today because they are moving the new hot water cylinder into the cellar. I join in thinking I can help prevent two men being crushed under a quarter of a ton of steel. Andrée appears, then Bob Gilbert, then two from Davis and Greenham to put a socket into the dining room for the new hot-plates: the era of paraffin lamps, and problems associated, is over. Bartletts come to fix the burst hydrant. Heather and Jeff are there anyway; so it only needs Caroline and Roy Copp for the team photograph.

Bob and I join David Puzey to look at a new burst in the field below the reservoir. David does some fancy work with his divining rod and confirms it is the house water supply, about 4 feet down. We then go up to inspect the wells feeding the Marsh Farm supply. Bob follows the water points down while I get a lift back with Michael Fooks.

Mr and Mrs Suddards arrive to look at the cottage again. Mercifully the heating is on and Bob says the damp is chiefly condensation and should dry out. We all have sherry with my father who is not in a conversational mood. Perhaps it is because Harold Macmillan's memorial service is on TV. I remind him that although he was his brother-in-law he chose not to attend it. But he has no regrets. After all, he says, 'I never got on with him and I did go up for Winston's'. Good boy.

Over to Piddletrenthide in the sun with Lady Anne Boyle – a painting of the 1st Earl's daughter-in-law, much praised by Pepys as an excellent match. She needs restoration after water from a burst pipe dripped on to her little finger. On the way I pick up a wayfarer and take him a mile along to Batcombe. He looks in the back and asks, 'not a Renoir or anything like that?' I say 'no, nothing like that' (just School of Lely). I deliver Lady Anne to Squire Jeffers, a restorer who shares a manor house and studio with his daughter. I'm tempted by the signpost outside his gate to go to Plush, and return by one of my roundabout routes via Cerne and Wraxall.

At dinner my father brings up the old chestnut about Luke putting in for the South Dorset seat and me going to the House of Lords. I said I hadn't finally made up my mind [I had more or less, but wouldn't tell him] and he said, 'oh but you have to, you don't have any choice; you wouldn't want to go into the Commons now, it wouldn't be worth it!' A generous way of looking at it.

Thursday 12th February

Over to Gray's Farm to meet an 'environmental sculptor' who wants to buy nine-foot posts, stretch blankets between them and set fire to them. He says at least he'll have the photographic record! On to Bridport via Eggardon and Spyway, with fine views through the mist. In search of an office equipment firm to service a typewriter, I get lost in two trading estates by the canal which remind me of Calcutta.

Walk down to Mythe to see the snowdrops, then on to the Leggs. Nearly get marooned in slurry but finally make it to the farmhouse. Maureen and Gordon want to get their big field limed but the contractors are unwilling to risk their machines; they also wonder if any of the government's new woodland grants could go their way. Down at Loscombe Derek Andrewes and I go through the list of stalls for the fair. Through his delightful wood and more snowdrops, then up the steep valley behind Jack's Hill. A few pigeons and pheasants get up, a deer breaks cover. Eerie twilight as the moon rises and I walk past four astonished sheep – no one passes them at this time except poachers. A week ago, according to George, a three-legged deer came out of the wood here carrying a snare on its fourth stump.

'Oh there you are, I was getting a little worried.' My father seems a bit dozy this evening and is off his food. There are signs of a spilled and broken sherry glass, and he drops off in front of the nine o'clock news which is rare. When I comment, he stays up for the ten o'clock.

Friday 13th February

Breakfast is quite a contrast with last night. I give myself a larger piece of fish and he notices. 'I think I'll have two eggs as you have the larger fish.' He then relents and gives up the second one, also offering an uneaten half of toast. I decline, having collected Ryvita from the sideboard; but regret it.

The line–up of visitors today: The Tolmans 3, Davis and Greenham (switches) 2, British Telecom (fresh from the strike) 2, Bill Duke and son (to remove wiring) 2, carpet cleaners 2, DCC Health Department 1, Richard Ashdown (firewood) 1, plus Andrée, Jane, Heather, Mr and Mrs Clark, my father and me. 20 of us in all.

All the carpets are superbly cleaned and refitted. Then a visit from Mr Smart the mole man, who describes how he introduces strychnine via worms into the more established holes, not the fresh ones; apparently the older ones have food storage. His bill has gone up from £5 to £25 – mainly the petrol from Gillingham. The Jacob's sheep are back in the big field opposite and Michael Fooks asks if we will turn over any sheep we see lying on their backs.

Saturday 14th February

Spend most of last night worrying about what to say to the Ways today about their possible move from Keepers Cottage. It's such a long and involved history there seems no way out! I go over and in the end we at least had a fair exchange of views and no one lost their temper.

The 'minor' shoot comes out in force and we spend most of the day clearing the new copse behind Daniell's garden. George and Nigel bulldoze the cut brambles down to the bonfire. Martin Rawstorne cuts his eye, I get very scratched, but the fire blazes and the dogs scramble happily around all day.

In the evening about 40 come to the shoot dinner. Big log fire and a delicious salmon and roulade prepared by Louisa who as usual takes things almost too calmly and carries the heaviest loads.

My father took two looks at the crowd and opted for the library, where the Scotts and Joan Best visited him. To bed by 1 am.

Monday 16th February

I collected the boys from Crewkerne and we all had a lovely two days before I took them back to Marlborough. We went to the Spyway Inn near Eggardon after a quick look at my parents' old log cabin site at Drakenorth with Higgy. It's nice to be able to say I was 'conceived at Heaven's Gate', which is the clump of beeches nearby. We drove back through Loders. In the evening we all went to 'Crocodile Dundee' in Yeovil, Luke – now 17 – doing most of the driving skilfully and firmly.

Two inches of snow settle during the night, but then melt in Tuesday's sun.

Sunday 22nd February

The last of the snow lingered under north–facing walls as I arrived for the weekend with Mima and her friend Nicola. Jean–Alice and Chris Koch came to discuss the parish meeting. Alice Powell couldn't make it as Dick is unwell in hospital. C and I had a very happy afternoon attacking the ivy and chatting. Higgy is cheered by her and the girls – great relief after days of me.

Sunday lunch today at Mangerton, where we meet Eve McKinnon who remembers Mapperton garden opening in the 1920s attended by smart London architects. There was a Hereford stately home owner who admits to running 'a terrible pile with a deer fence'. Iona comes back to help with the ivy, while Robin Mangles and other minor day guns continue to clear brambles on the hill. Bob comes about the kitchen conversion, our great Gordian knot still uncut. We decide to abandon the dresser (later rescinded) and to make a new ford to replace the collapsed bridge below Burcombe.

Monday 23rd February

Today does not turn out as expected. Few days here do. I plan to write up Christian Aid Indo–China projects. First, my father suggests an outing to Bridport to find a hot–plate and is disappointed when I refuse, a bit abruptly. I had sudden memories of being unable to refuse in the past. A firm called Technicon turn up to relag the pipes, and they promptly get locked out of the back door. The pond is choked with flannel weed, so Jeff comes in to phone a pond expert at Kingston Maurward. Then I spot Jacob's sheep escaping through the hedge just cleared by the shoot, but manage to head them back again.

Finally I abandon all hope of my own work in favour of helping Jeff with the pond. Together we push great pools of sludge down the sluice, rescuing the goldfish with a net and bucket. Andrew, Patsy's son, watches and helps – it's his birthday, and he'll remember this for ever. Two fish, possibly more, die and disappear down the stream but over 20 are saved. Jeff's stutter makes him difficult to follow but he is very good company and poses complex questions about overseas aid and its ineffectiveness, which I try to answer.

In between, Gemma comes to lunch and reminds me that other establishments are having difficulty paying bills. My father at first forgets he's got a niece at all – 'Oh yes, of course, Faith's daughter'. It's nice for me that she hears all the tedious repetitions as well as his more mellow style, no longer dominating.

The hot water boiler is out again and I still smell of sludge.

Wednesday 25th February

Farce breaks out when I ask Mr Kennedy's opinion of copper sulphate as a treatment for flannel weed. He pooh–poohs the expert advice: 'What you need is a couple of ducks, they'll eat it up in no time, that's what they did at Mrs Dilke's.' Incontrovertible, except for the lurking fox. Meanwhile my father and I are chasing each other round the house, me locked out of the front door and the office, the key mislaid, and him unusually emerging from the back door, perhaps on my advice.

Michael Fooks comes across the garden to look at the shoot's proposal to feed pheasants in a corner of the top Holeacre field above the garden spinney. We place a large white stone as a boundary. He is now going to move his sheep back to Poorton for lambing.

A young organist comes up for tea and to look at the church. I am ashamed to show the harmonium to someone who has apparently been playing for months in the cathedral in Jerusalem, but he sits down and fills the church with the most wonderful sounds. The old machine can't be too bad after all.

Thursday 26th February

Rain sets in. The golden orfe are still in the trough so I give them buckets of water and fish meal. Only one corpse found this morning. I go into Bridport and get a trim from Jack the hairdresser who is like Mr Miles with his clippers in Huntingdon in the Fifties. Have a drink with Simon Dorrington–Ward in the George. Back home I start on an article on Kampuchea before going out to the Home–Smiths for dinner in thick fog. Coming back I can hardly recognise our own road and nearly run down a white deer and a black dog. Watch Robin Day on Question Time and then at the Greenwich by–election. This resulted from the death of Guy Barnett, previously Labour member for South Dorset, elected after my father famously split the Tory vote in 1962.

Friday 27th February

Rain still heavy but after breakfast I collect a pressure washer from Able's and get down to the pool with the Kennedys. It takes us two hours to connect plugs and hoses, using Joyce's extension lead run down from the Garden Cottage. Mr K curses at every turn but is skilful at fixing while I almost despair at my lack of tools and plumbing skills. He finally says at lunchtime, 'It's a very good machine,' and why didn't we buy one (at over £500 compared to £17 for the day). Jeff will be pleased to find the pool cleaned and refilled. Steve Davis, the electrician, returns our old fire nozzle that he wanted to show the fire brigade. The Kennedys finally get fed up and abandon everything to me and the drizzle. Mima and C turn up for a non–supper and we slump in front of poor TV.

Saturday/Sunday 28-29 March

We all drive off in the Peugeot to Scott's to pick up plants. The sun is trying to cheer us up but doesn't quite. Caroline has started a new collection of abandoned plant labels and is matching them with the splendid plant record book my father has 'found' on his desk.

I show him the new garden advertisement we've put in the *Echo*: 'Splendid,' he said, 'How did I do that?' He normally does it. I explained that Andrée had drawn the griffins and I had written the text.

He's bothered about <u>very</u> small things which come round and round at meals and make some moments unbearable, especially when I am on my own. This week it has been enough firewood under the stairs, which always starts a chain of questions about Richard Ashdown and when he is going to do this, that or the other.

Hubbards to dinner which is lovely for both of us. C takes them round the garden in floodlight. Matins in Melplash on Sunday, Mima and I back home – to London.

Wednesday 4th March

Snowing again in London, just enough to cover roofs. Overnight drama at Mapperton unfolds on the telephone. Patsy decided to take an overdose after SWEB cut off her electricity. Luckily she rang the Ways and was taken to Yeovil hospital, having arranged for a social worker to pick up the children; apparently no one is usually that thoughtful.

I decide to go down in the evening though it seems only to show a flag – not many of those are being run up at the moment. When I arrive I find Helen with a torch saying Patsy was home, had had a meal and was now asleep. The social worker has left a helpful answer–phone message saying she had discharged herself in the afternoon.

My father keeps asking about the court hearing which will free the flat for Shirley (our new housekeeper). He said it wouldn't have been the first time someone had died in the house, what about Mrs Labouchere? The conversation – over two delicious woodcock we couldn't eat – turned to our old friends the Lyles in Scotland, and the possibility of them coming for a shoot in the autumn. He said he doubted he would still be there, and anyway he was 81 in May and didn't shoot any more. I said that having survived the last terrible winter he could survive several more.

He nodded off in the library, possibly liquor or relief that I am there, and almost dropped his glasses. He reached out for the TV control and I managed to get there before he lurched out of the Dutch burgomaster's chair on to the floor. I started wondering how long 'self–reliance' would last.

Thursday 5th March

Fine sunny day as I collect the newspapers – another job inherited. Alice Powell tells me Dick may be moved from Weymouth to Bridport to convalesce after his op; Alf says Joyce is now walking outside a bit and plans to come to the coffee morning; paper rounds can bring good news. Above the office come peals of laughter and bloody this and that from Ethel: I even saw Patsy knitting, coming rather quickly back to life. We must get SWEB to turn the power on.

My father and I chug over to Poorton in the Chevette to see the Fooks family. As usual the whole family appears from nowhere. Edna shows us a lovely photographic book of Dorset by Jo Draper. Alan hobbles off – he is due for a hip op – and we follow him into the field to see four new–born lambs. One is being bottle–fed. The barns look perfectly stacked with bales and everything tidily arranged in stalls. Back in time to see Bob Ahrens of the cadets about a Duke of Edinburgh Award scheme.

Friday 6th March

A man comes to fit an aerial on the roof of Garden Cottage, climbs up and finds one already installed. Someone has boobed, but no one owns up – least of all Caroline. Mr and Mrs Stanford come up about the Suffolk Punch and I buy a raffle ticket which would get me dinner for two in Chedington Court – where Sir Geoffrey Peto, MP for Chard, one of Mum's many uncles, lived. Very cold wind blowing through the yard. I spend the evening on an article for *Christian Aid News* until C arrives late with the hot plates. Finally the paraffin lamp era is over; we sit up until after midnight fitting new plugs.

Saturday 7th March

At breakfast Higgy ignores, or fails to notice, the hotplates. You can't blame him as they are like sleek black cats, merging successfully with the sideboard. The weather is still foul but we manage to get out to the goldfish pool, where George has unblocked the drain down the gully. Mr K has still not reconnected the tap by the lower pool (I can't).

Higgy and I go into Bridport to visit Dick in hospital. I dropped him there and went shopping for 20 minutes, came back and he was gone. The nurses were confused while I searched the garden and WCs, and then Dick said he must have 'gone on'. I caught him up nearly half a mile away by the post office. We both apologized. I was late and he had obviously got bored listening to some old gaffer describing the view of West Bay.

Michael and Ann Hudson come to dinner. He has been our family doctor for years. We have a warm fire in the drawing room, delicious pheasant for supper, and learn they are going off to find lemurs in Madagascar.

Sunday 8th March

C is feeling bilious, and I have that dispirited ebbing in the stomach which often goes with Mapperton on her departure days – what a pair we make. Canadian XBX army exercises boost morale and circulation. Another dull day, mainly in the office. The Bests have cancelled coming to lunch, but I only remembered after Shirley had cooked two chickens. Hot water on again – oh for a lovely bath.

Monday 9th March

00.30 am: the alarm goes off. I turn it off but the bell continues ringing and the siren on the roof whooshes! I take refuge in the kitchen and phone Shorrocks. I wake Higgy but he goes straight back to sleep. The bell eventually stops; apparently the alarm phone is out of order anyway. I explain this to my father hours later over the grapefruit marmalade. He says, frowning, 'Who are the bells ringing for, anyway?' The burglars, I suggested. But neither Heather nor Joyce had heard anything. Later Alice said she remembered the first time the alarm went off: Michael the former gardener was there with a stick and Dick stood in the drive with a shotgun, with Alf and Joyce following on – all that was left of the feudal militia.

Jeff has planted the new winter flowering cherry, just above the old one at the head of the gully. It looks lovely, reminding us of Albert Bridge Road. Jim White has been in to level the path. It's a sunny but cold day. I walk up from Melplash after dropping the car, bicycling back in the evening. Touchingly my father appears in the office: 'I thought you might have fallen off your bicycle, I'm so relieved you're back...'

Thursday 12th March

James Lang Brown arrives on the dot of 10 a.m. I am frantically trying to clean the office, shoo the stray Jacob's sheep through the fence and make myself a salami sandwich. We start planning the new trees in the 'park' across the ha—ha where Luke wants a cedar. Dick, just back home, reminds us he's already planted one. We settle for chestnuts and a copper beech.

Disaster at Drakenorth: deer have chewed off 80% of the new Scotch pine. We sight about 10 fallows and James abandons all hope of planting until we can control them. Mr Crees' cows have also broken through, up the steep slope above the old log cabin site. Luckily the beeches are OK. On to David Fooks to see the field he wants to buy. They have a lamb in a cardboard box mauled by a fox. Walk on down to Burcombe, chat with Julian Gordon Watson, then follow the pleached hedge down to Mythe and up through Home Wood. Les and Ethel are rounding up their geese which is comic, and I follow to see their eggs laid in a hutch. Back to Wytherston for supper. Discussing others' problems is a great distraction. I still feel ridiculously tied to Mapperton.

Friday 13th March

Our first two Jacob's lambs appear with the first daffodils and primroses, but it's still cold. My father is having gramophone trouble. I once caught him pushing down the needle to increase the volume. As a result an electrician regularly gets £10 just to flick a switch.

We drive Betts, now in her own flat in Battersea Park, down for the weekend and visit Bill's new cottage in the Somerset Levels. Patsy's children are back and she is all over the *Bridport News*.

Monday 16th March

Spend most of the day in the office: Courtyard Fair and some editing work. The sheep get out again. Perhaps as bribes, I agree to collect four more bags of sheep nuts from Mosterton Mill — a gloomy complex awaiting redevelopment. My father agrees to pay for path levelling, then generously suggests I mow the paths for him. 'I used to do it about this time, but I don't feel really interested any more.' I have mixed emotions: gratitude, to some extent; horror, at the scope of the task; sadness, that he is relinquishing it. Perhaps he'll forget he has. He falls asleep in front of the TV, which is now standard. I can't get used to his assumption that nothing has changed in the house, even the small things. 'Leave the dishes, Heather will clear away,' even though she has long gone home and I've been washing up since Christmas. It can't be deliberate, or can it? – one can never be sure. I can't help thinking he prefers guests who come – and go. But he simply has to recognize that we are living here in our own right, not at his discretion.

St Patrick's Day breakfast

THE CAST Higgy, the disgruntled peer, also known as
HINCH; John, the restless heir
THE SCENE: Dining–room
THE DATE: March 17th 1987

JOHN: *(cautiously):* Morning.

HIGGY: *(bright today):* Good morning. I've only just started. Help yourself!

JOHN: Warmer today. There might be some daffodils out.

HIGGY: *(cross):* Yes. I wish Heather would cut off the bacon rinds. I must tell her. Is she still here?

JOHN *(RELIEVED):* No, she's gone. By the way, we've got the coffee morning today.

HIGGY: This grapefruit marmalade's awfully good. I wonder where it comes from. Pines?

JOHN: You and I got it together in Cerne Abbas. Do you want any more toast?

HIGGY *(WORRIED):* Oh yes of course, you told me. I'll see if Pines has got it. I wanted to tell you the sheep have been getting out again, that copse where the shoot have cut the brambles...

JOHN: I'll go and see. The Fooks should be coming soon to move them to the Rectory orchard. They're hungry and they've no more grass left.

HIGGY *(AGITATED):* Have you asked the Rectory, who's in the Rectory. Have they moved in yet? (Pause) Who's in the Lower Garden Cottage? How much rent are they paying? What's their name? Oh yes you told me. (Pause) The man's coming to mend the gramophone again.

JOHN: Didn't he come yesterday?

HIGGY: Yes he did but there's still – a fault. I don't know what's the matter with it. I can't get it to work. I have to pay him £10 each time. I rang him up again this morning. If you see a man lurking in the house, he's coming to mend the gramophone. Oh well, I must go and get the papers, do you need anything in the town?

JOHN *(WEARY):* It's all right, I got the papers before breakfast.

HIGGY *(DISAPPOINTED):* Oh. You did? Oh...well, thank you very much. I think I'll go and finish off [recording] the weather. Will you ring the Fooks? By the way if you see a man lurking about he's coming to mend my gramophone... (EXITS TOWARDS THE LIBRARY)

The Coffee Morning

St Patrick's Day, and the long-awaited coffee morning. The air is warmer. The phone rings: will I please collect Peggy Fairall whose car battery is flat (and 'Nancy', and pot plants and jumble)? Bobby arrives with convalescent Elaine: farmers' wives bustle about with tables and coffee cups and sticky labels. My father is dressed in a smart brown suit, having stopped asking if the event's being held in the village hall. I ask him for an old hat for raffle tickets and he says his hats are rather good (they are), but I shall go and look for one in the loo. I collect a Tyrolean one the minute he disappears. Jemima is wrongly accused by him of eating biscuits specially bought for today, but Shirley finds more. A sheet just covers the dining-room table. Christian Koch, our very obliging Anglican friend, arrives and tries to blow damp logs – in vain. Shirley and Stan collect 30ps from the first arrivals.

Over 60 people pour in. Bobby and Peggy carry steaming cups while I help Chris with the bellows. The time comes for the draw but Andrée says she's just seen my father in Beaminster Square. How did he get there? Oh well. I draw the tickets and he wins chocolates, Jane wins a doll and Alice a bottle. Joyce and I stay till the end. By midday everyone has gone and I'm exhausted.

No breakages. My father wanders in for a sherry, removes logs
and the smoke drives us all away.

Friday 20th March

Back from London by train, passing through snow–bound Southampton
into glorious sunny East Dorset – delayed 40 minutes but collect the
Chevette at Dorchester and arrive just in time for (1.15) lunch.

Everything is sweetness and light today. The eviction party set
out for Dorchester exactly on time and was duly received in the
County Court. Patsy said she and my father sat down on a bench
together and waited opposite some extended family doing the same,
all wondering what the others were in for. Higgy said the proceedings
were all over in under half an hour, and they drove home through
Bridport. 'I used to go over the old Roman road but I don't like to
go that way now because if you break down there are no garages. I
used to know it very well.'

The solicitor from Creech and Co hints that all may not be as
well as we think because Patsy, having resigned, is not in the same
deserving category as the 'real' eviction cases. This means we will
have to be cruel to be kind, or we shall all be in a Catch–22. C feels
strongly about this and we had two difficult telephone conversations.

We went to look at the sheep, back in the Rectory orchard, happily
grazing on real grass again. I show my father the general plan for the
stable conversion and explain for the umpteenth time that it cannot
affect the Rectory tenancy. Then I show him round the ground floor
of the Rectory, newly decorated, which we both admire.

Monday–Tuesday 23rd-24th March

A miserable drizzle and fog – the very worst sort of Dorset day,
enough to dampen the enthusiasm of toads in the lower garden. Jeff
Truscott decides it is not a good day for him and anyway he has
a heavy cold. Monday is the first day of the Community Play in

Beaminster which features a Mapperton magistrate and a couple of ghost children played by the Gordon Watson girls – we are going to it next week.

I have tea and a long talk with Dick and Alice about the future. Clearly Dick would like to go on working for the estate – he sniffs at all other options I put in front of him ('I'm only telling you what the possibilities are, Dick') but jumps at the idea of making a table for the old school hall or for the Courtyard Fair while on the estate payroll. At one moment he suggested getting a whole set of woodworking tools but I restrained him on the grounds that he is used to the old tools. We have a delicious cup of tea and biscuit and he reminisced about the time he was foreman of the entire estate. 'What have you done with all your men?' I teased him. At one time he had all the gardeners as well as the foresters under him, and now he is the only one left.

'Would you like to see my guns?' Dick said suddenly and I gratefully follow Alice upstairs to look at his .22 and his 12 bore. I wish Luke were here to make a proper assessment. I walk back down in the rain, looking at the Jacob's sheep and wondering why only two lambs have appeared.

The courtyard fair meeting, its agenda now computerised, proceeds well although we still have no news about the helicopter. Portland will probably have a fit when they hear my new whistled tune on the answerphone: 'Speed Bonny Boat'.

Wednesday 1st April

Arrived at Crewkerne station to find the Vauxhall battery *kaput* at 10pm. Asparagus soup in the pub until a patient AA man arrives. He starts the car three times but it keeps stalling and he follows me back to our turning. No sign of life, but the lights are all on and the front door open. Eventually Orlando turns up with Duncan Forbes and we have a midnight feast.

Thursday–Friday 2nd-3rd April

Two of the wettest, windiest days imaginable. The Suddards, just arrived at the Garden Cottage from Windsor, don't seem to mind as they are busy unpacking and creating a home. The decorators had just got out in time, but then unfortunately a window fell out and a loo began to leak. Deadlines simply don't agree with Mapperton.

My father is in a state about an MOT and licence for the Range Rover. He started out for Beaminster on Friday without even finishing his breakfast – egg half-eaten, toast and coffee untouched – to present himself to the postmaster. In the yard I tried to put his papers in order, the rain beating down; he had left his keys behind. Finally he came back with a new licence, pretending all had been well from the start. I gave him a *pâté de canard* which Mum had bought him in France. She wrote a note with a Cole Porter song and a suggested plant which he threw straight into the wpb. I fished it out later, as I have got used to doing, to save important letters being lost.

Sunday 5th April

Shirley arrived late as she had passed David Way in his car in the ditch on Jack's Hill, apparently after a good Saturday night out, but he comes to and seems all right. The police are taking care of him and there are licence problems too.

Still no house available for Patsy, so Shirley and Stan have to be patient again. Mr Davenport of the WDDC has more or less promised 'bed and breakfast' for her when the court order runs out and we are entitled to call the bailiff at Easter.

Mohamed Ali, the ram, continues to jump out of the orchard and there is much talk of taking him to market. Gary Way came past and got a fiver for chasing him back.

Caroline and the children have come for the week – our first holiday together since Christmas. The rain continues but we get out for an hour of pruning.

Monday 6th April

'Darling how is it we have managed to give Heather a week's holiday when Mrs Clark is off.' We grit our teeth. Shirley isn't off, she is simply not on, and we are managing fine, though not without difficulty, i.e. when Orlando refuses to come down to start homework after watching videos all night.

Alarm this evening: the flue from the central heating belches fumes which steal through a plate in the office wall. We are nearly asphyxiated investigating it, and ring Tolmans to say we won't be there to pay their bills if they don't come. The next morning the air is as pure as the Himalayas.

But of course it won't last, and hundreds will have to be spent relining it.

Tuesday 12th May

A fox appeared on the hill, trotting round the field where the Jacob's are grazing undisturbed. Mohamed Ali would have seen him off but was chasing younger ewes next door. Mrs Higgins rings up almost daily to complain but no solution has emerged.

Mrs Thatcher has declared a General Election for June 11th. My father has missed the boat: he was going to write and remind her that Baldwin said Conservatives usually win an autumn election.

The garden is settling into the elegance of early summer, the grass growing too fast even for Jeff to keep up. The Talbots, Roy and Elizabeth, came to Sunday lunch and said how lovely the shrubs were looking. After 30 years my father is at last seeing the glory of the garden he has created; we are even finding his old labels, on which Caroline has done a lot of work. He still talks of mowing and has done some in the orchard, though his beloved garden paths are now largely over to Jeff. He is fussing about – well, what does it matter, he'll always fuss about something. Mr K has urged me to water seeds, tomato plants, young vegetables and above all the lavender cuttings but I haven't got around them all. I have, however, mown the car park and the drive verges with the Kubota.

An American wrestler turned Devon Buddhist gave a talk in Beaminster church last night. He gets up at 4 every morning and spends the first hour in silence, saying it's the best time of all; I believe him. But he says he has a problem with the mosquitoes.

Mum has had a terrible car accident near Montpellier from which she is recovering in hospital, and we have all been out in relays to see her. Julia and Renée were with her; in spite of injuries they have been discharged.

Patsy at last agreed, with strong persuasion from Caroline and others, to move down to a flat in Beaminster. Shirley and Stan have moved into the flat and although it isn't ready the atmosphere has already calmed down. Even the yard has brightened up with shrubs and they've painted the front door. We can start talking sensibly about the security of the house. Tomorrow we have two parties going round and the Clarks are going to help with them. Shirley and Stan went to Saturday's parish meeting, and she is helping with coffee for today's courtyard fair meeting.

Caroline is finishing a Middle East report. Somehow when she isn't here the various contractors stay away and I am not encouraging them to come. Yet the jackdaws are settling into the library chimney (my father tried to smoke them out while Douglas Jay was visiting), the bonfire is piling up, trees need attention, the flat needs a fireplace, and as usual everywhere you look something needs doing.

Saturday 16th May

This morning showers have given way to warm sun which is drying out the garden. I spent five minutes on the grass bank by the lead herons, taking in the scene. Bullocks charging across the lynchets (mediaeval terraces) and then staring over the gate at the sheep. The postman driving up to Holeacre where the Higgins are collecting their own sheep – Mohamed Ali is rumoured to have mouth disease.

My father, driving a newly–repaired Range Rover back from Bridport to see beloved Fiona (Nickals) and family who are staying. All around the sounds of animals: yapping (Shirley's terriers), bleating, birds chattering, a cuckoo, and the odd pheasant honking.

In the library chimney the jackdaws are busy rebuilding the nest Alf swept clear on Thursday: my father telephoned the Copps four times apparently. It will need scaffolding or long ladders to put a grille round the chimney pot.

Two nights ago I saw another fox, red–brown and grey, ambling along the road to Marsh Farm, then slipping down the field beside the stream.

I've spent most of the week in the office: the fair, the estate and the house have taken up the time and I haven't started my London work – it's very hard to justify it when there is so much to be done around you. Yesterday I spent an hour clearing the pond of flannel weed, but it is still half covered. I have cut the verges, but there is plenty more to do with the strimmer, on the drive and down the garden.

On Wednesday a party of 43 came from Barnet to see the house and garden. The Clarks were very helpful. They divided into two groups and I gave them the standard tour which starts: 'At the time of the Domesday Book Mapperton earned William de Moion, Sheriff of Somerset, an income of 70 shillings.' I'm getting better at it, but I'm blowed if I know anything about the stained glass or the objects in the church and find myself fudging the answers terribly. Where can one find the time to sit down with Hutchins' History of Dorset and references in the library – and with my father groaning occasionally that he would really rather no one came into the house at all?

Sunday 23rd May

Mrs Clark went to get the papers this morning and left my father a note, but I strongly suspect he has gone down for them again. Jackdaws are twittering around the chimney above the dining room – a family which Roy Copp decided to leave alone for a few weeks until they grew older and would either fly or fall out. He went up the long ladder to the library chimney stack on Friday – a good 70 feet above a sheer drop down the west wall – and put his hand through a hole in the grille and pulled out a fat jackdaw like a boy in a nursery rhyme. 'Now then, you behave yourself,' he said, tapping it on the nose and putting it in his pocket before making the journey down.

A red–faced road mender drew up in a Merc last week with an impressive gang of four and a lorry and stories of work done all over the county. My father said yes, he would like the potholes filled. The next thing he saw was half the drive resurfaced and a four–figure bill. I arrived with the boys just as it was being presented. My father was driving off to Salisbury for the night, oblivious of what we had to sort out. The man came back the next day, but I managed to put him off until Tuesday.

Tuesday 25th May

The man in the Merc duly returned this morning to demand his money. Luckily I had paced the area with Bob Gilbert during the weekend and had his opinion that a) he was overcharging even on the work carried out and b) his tarmac wasn't properly sealed anyway and would admit rainwater and crack up. This gave me the confidence to pay not a penny more than the original estimate for potholes already budgeted under the estate account, so I paid him a cheque for £300 and said he would have to talk to my father about any additional payment. Meanwhile I had briefed my father to prepare a £100 goodwill payment which I eventually handed over with much ceremony. He tried all sorts of ploys on me such as 'surely you wouldn't want an old pair of trousers patched up, you'd want a new pair wouldn't you?' A story about his own elderly father backfired because he obviously hadn't the courage to push the original sum. At a crucial moment my father happened to walk out and the man called out, 'Mr Montagu, you're an honourable man surely?' Luckily the reply came back smartly: 'I'm not paying you any more than I already have done.' My father continued to walk past him across the yard with superb, if unpredictable timing. The wretched man drove away with only one–tenth of what he wanted, and maybe West Dorset is the safer for it. The *Echo*, at Caroline's instigation, ran a lead front–page story on it the following week, luckily without mentioning any names.

Friday 19th June

The last month has been much quieter thanks to the presence of Shirley and Stan Clark who are becoming wholly dependable caretakers. This morning I am down for the regular courtyard fair meeting – one of the windiest and nastiest June days on record. The beech tree on the far bank made a roaring sound like a waterfall and I hope it stays up. A nice Morris dancer came up to talk about the fair and turns out to be a friend of Jeff's and a chorister at Pilsdon.

My father was turning over his diary pages this afternoon and found a note of some friends who were to call in on Tuesday, either for lunch or for the night. I suggested he give them a ring to check it out, but he said why not wait till they come, 'and see if they bring suitcases – and then we'll know'. I've noticed that he understandably takes the line of least resistance and hopes that all will be well on the day (they never came). Yet he still wants to be in the know and aware of what is happening, which is a blessing and a curse for smooth arrangements on the estate if the telephone happens to ring. The other day a man came up to do some fencing, apparently recommended to him, but luckily Shirley spotted him and told us.

Friday 26th June

This morning my father was distinctly off colour and couldn't eat any kedgeree, only a half-piece of toast and marmalade. Lunch was the same but he had perked up a bit. We walked round the house and looked at an elder growing under the church east window, deciding to remove it. He suggested Mr Kennedy but I said both gardeners were over-occupied with weeding and grass-cutting and I said I would take a saw to it. We dropped in on the pigeoncote and found remains of birds disappearing into guano: worth mentioning to Mr K in case he can use any of it.

A nice feature about the house in the *Echo* this week – gently encouraging group visits to see the ceilings and naval collection. My father seems pleased with it and raises no objections – he's more worried about the Round Table summer ball and which bedroom to retreat to.

Friday 3rd July

My father met me at Crewkerne yesterday. He was feeling mildly better: Dr Hudson has tried to provide antibiotics in between the cocktails, so we can't blame them for not working.

The weather is, at last, warm and sunny. The Fooks brothers are taking the hay off the two opposite fields, but with the heavy rain last week the goodness was washed out of it. They have baled it and are now lifting heavy 48–bale stacks up to the barn at Holeacre, still working until around 10 p.m. last night when everyone else was settling down to Chris Evert and Navratilova in the semi–final. I spent an hour and a half on the flannel weed, which is at last tameable on the bed of the upper pool. I am about one-third down the pool, and get some enjoyment out of the tadpoles, as though I was still damming the beach at Bembridge. Last time I was down there a line of garden visitors formed up behind the wall, so I am thinking of charging for entertainment.

At about 7.20 p.m. I managed to get the garden tractor and trailer up to the bonfire, heavily loaded with stinking weed, and found a cloud of flies were pursuing me into supper. A very rapid bath on borrowed time, so I got into the dining–room only to find my father halfway through his heap of fishbones passing for plaice, washed down with acid Burgundy and Thousand Island dressing. It took one phone call about 10 minutes later (Gemma sadly announcing my aunt

Betts' having gone to hospital just before her 70th birthday party) and the meal was over. You have to get used to this at Mapperton now – harder because of the memory of more luxurious evenings, like the ones with two courses and cheese, even second helpings!

He is, of course, forgetful like all octogenarians. Sometimes in the evenings with plenty of sherry or vodka he will ramble into childish responses like 'bless you' which becomes 'bess you' or 'besh you' which can be irritating or touching, depending on your own mood. He occasionally goes into recurring questions like 'Caroline coming down?' or 'Like some port?' which can come back literally seconds later so you have to think quickly of diversionary tactics. He also repeats the word 'yes' three times which is usually a prelude to 'Can you ask me tomorrow?' or 'We'll look at it in the morning' – a great relief all round.

I waver between wanting to keep him fully informed – which has practical advantages as well as occupying his mind – and keeping the information from him at all costs, knowing the ghastly sequences and often irrational thought processes which will follow. It's not just a question of the time of day and amount of alcohol, because he sometimes shows remarkable clarity and resilience and I find I even have to restrain a longing to share problems and experiences and probably err on the sharing side, rather than use up some of my own sanity.

He is forgetting who is who in the family, not surprisingly if you think of the numbers and combinations involved. Yesterday I told him about the difficulties our niece Caterina was in, borrowing money from friends of ours in Bombay, and he couldn't imagine who I was taking about and I was naughtily tempted to let him try. 'Faith's daughter?' But when I told him he remembered her, which is amazing, considering how long she has been away. He sometimes gets Julia and Betts the wrong way round, so that when I say Betts is coming down he asks rather comically whether she is bringing (Julia's son) Timmy.

What concerns us all a bit is that such is his reputation for parking the Range Rover against walls and other cars he is one day going to do himself and other people some damage. He loves driving, but I am trying to encourage a smaller car in which Shirley Clark could sometimes drive him. Not surprisingly I'm having absolutely no success, but with luck PC Dawson will grab him one of these days.

Sunday 12th July

Left alone after the weekend my father and I often show a sort of infectious wariness. We stalk through the house peering round corners in case of wild beasts of prey coming out on us. Anything as inoffensive as Shirley or Heather passing through, or Jane dusting, is likely to make us start. Suspicion is not far behind. I arrived first at breakfast this morning and was on the alert from the moment my father left the staircase hall on his way to the dining-room. There is a point where a man standing by the toaster can detect another man's movement at the far end of the sitting-room. From then on, eye-to-eye combat is inevitable, lids raised and lowered every few seconds during his shambling arrival. A long pause while the ground is marked out. 'Morning.' 'Morning.' And from then on: 'Morello cherry?' 'No thank you, marmalade,' and the battle is joined.

Earlier I had walked through to the gramophone room to return the pliers to the tool box. Inadvertently I carried the office key which is normally never seen further north than the kitchen door. Footsteps were coming through the sitting-room, and I walked boldly out to meet them.

'Ah-ha!' 'Ah-ha! Hello,' we called, grinning like vultures. He catches sight of the key. 'What's that key?' 'It's the office key.' 'Oh, does it belong in the gramophone room?' 'No, I've just been returning the pliers.' 'Pliers?' From then on all is sublime, anything is credible, all of us are culpable. One can only pray.

Yesterday at exactly the same crossroads my father passed through the remains of a debate between us and Orlando – essentially about whether his friends could come and practise pop music in the old saw mill. (In the end, the vocalist found a cowshed in Askerswell, but it was crucial at the time.) 'Hello. We're just having a family discussion,' we called tersely, and he took the point immediately. 'sandwiches at seven? Right,' he said, and passed on towards the drinks tray.

On Saturday we went to the tithe barn at Hinton St Mary, near Sturminster – a glorious setting with a Tuscan landscape looming above the hedges and between the trees – to hear the horn-player Barry Tuckwell, with Sheila Armstrong singing Richard Strauss and Donizetti. I suggested lightly to my father that, given half a million, we could convert the south stable into a superb concert hall, seating 300 at a pinch (I got the idea from Orlando's pop friends). In return I received only a half-smile, and deserved it. 'I think I should hear it through my bedroom window.' And well you might, just as you may possibly see the Morris dancers at the courtyard fair next month. The other side is double-glazed, which is why he heard nothing of the 450-strong Bridport Round Table Jubilee Ball band on Friday night, in a giant marquee only yards from his bedroom. In the end he was quite calm about this event, and impressed when they came to scavenge shreds of coloured streamers on Sunday afternoon.

Sunday 9th August

The Jacob's sheep are safely back in the Rectory orchard, thanks to the Fooks family's ingenuity. My father had rung Alan a fortnight ago to say he had had enough of them – could they be removed? C and I were in London, so they were taken back to Poorton – in any case the older ewes were due for the market. The Fooks' were well aware that another phone call might come: 'I can't think what can have happened to the sheep. Johnny, do you have any idea where they are?' and so they have smuggled them back as if nothing had happened. Even the dreaded Mohamed Ali is back, having escaped slaughter and the hobble and, worse, the wrath of Mrs Higgins protecting her ewes. He is happily chewing trees round the tennis court.

My father has a devastating new question which goes, 'What are we [we!] going to do about…' the sheep, Louis — Orlando's new Labrador puppy — or anything else he finds difficult, skilfully throwing responsibility on the nearest passer-by rather than himself.

Last Thursday night we all had a shock. He had gone into the library after dinner and twenty minutes later we heard him scuffling past the dining room door looking for us. His head was bleeding and there were spots of blood all down the passage.

Apparently he had fallen in the fireplace trying to turn off the switch, staggering and hurting his head on something sharp, perhaps the stone edge. I drove him down to Dr Wiley in Bridport hospital, to have five stitches. There was a screaming child with an alleged splinter next to him throughout, but he said later he hadn't noticed her. Meanwhile Caroline and Lando discovered smoke in the library and found charred floorboards beside an overturned electric fire, so it was a lucky escape in that department too. Back home, showing him the floor was like taking the puppy to his messes, with a similar minimal effect I guess. He seemed quite cheerful and started spreading ointment and dabbing water on his head, expressly against doctor's orders. (A week later Dr Hudson took out the stitches and amazingly his head seemed to clear up altogether.)

The puppy, like the cat, has become a focus of resentment. I think he resents almost anyone in the house after a certain interval, even his favourite guests. But he has also had his share of cleaning up the messes outside the library with remarkably good grace. He seems to have forgotten that dogs have to start as puppies. I said we all started like that but he said 'yes, in our nappies'.

More sheep in the garden this week, this time the Fooks' which have wandered up from the lower field. Caroline tells Pam firmly that they will have to take away the droppings too. Louis and I between us managed to head off one lot from the fountain court, herding them through a dangerously narrow exit by the blue gate. This was before 7 a.m. I'm up with Louis at 2 a.m. and 6 a.m. some mornings, and have started weeding the gravel path down to Garden Cottage as a ploy.

Orlando meanwhile is off to sunny Corfu, leaving his charge behind. They have a lot in common: mess, aggression, playful falling about and getting under everyone's feet. They should do each other good.

Monday 24th August

Last week Caroline's parents have been staying and the weather has been very warm. The Fooks family have cut both the Holeacre fields despite a breakdown of the harvester. Fountains Forestry are now thinning the plantation in earnest: I walked through there the other day and it smells delicious, like a vast German forest.

My father suddenly expressed a wish to go to Drakenorth. He said he felt very nostalgic for the log cabin which he hadn't seen for 30 years – now the standard way of saying, not for at least a week or two. We climbed into the Range Rover – this was Saturday and everyone else was out – carrying the picnic basket and drove along the Hooke road, running into Alan Fooks on the Poorton turning and having a chat with him. I thought when we got to Drakenorth he would miss the Douglas firs which have been felled – I almost wished he would – but he said nothing and gazed at the Eggardon horizon. 'Isn't that the Hardy monument over there?' The direction was right but I told him it was actually the wind–swept lone tree on Eggardon Hill. 'Who owns Eggardon? Didn't we have land here at one time? Who's maintaining the duck hides now? Powell used to do it.' I didn't have satisfactory answers to any of these questions, but we had a very relaxed picnic in a pool of sun above the lake. I think he thought we were close to the log cabin site, and I said we would come back another time with the children, and come in by the beeches at 'Heaven's Gate'. The log cabin itself has been long gone. Some boys got in and wee'd all over the mattresses for a joke, and Bill Guy says he was asked by Grandpa to burn them, and eventually to pull down the whole cabin which was obviously not used enough. I often think I started life there. There was a stove with a chimney but no water which was fetched from the stream. It was probably one of those basic camp sites which parents still enjoy at 35, before older children make it too difficult.

The fox, aided by badgers, got up to 50 of the new pheasants in Home Wood on their first night – ten per cent of the lot. The badgers dug the holes and fused the electric wire, and the fox helped himself. A bat got into the drawing room on Saturday evening, and we chased madly after it with flimsy butterfly and fishing nets, Perceval and Sylvia enjoying the spectacle. It was more bizarre because my father is endlessly grumbling about the windows being left open, if not about the cat and the new puppy, Louis. Caroline being determined to let as much air (partly metaphorical) into the house as possible; and that precise moment was the time he comes out of the library to go to bed. It was rather like stepping round the mess made by the labrador, playing musical doors between the hall and the drawing–room so that the bat – at last safely trapped in the larger net – would pass unnoticed.

All was well, but there was an unhappy ending of which we were then unaware, with my father staggering upstairs and unable to put on his pyjamas, then falling and cutting himself again, on the arm this time. Caroline only found blood on the shirt the next day when he told me about it. He was probably tired out by the picnic and house guests, but alcohol comes a close third. I told him he didn't have to get into the pyjamas if he was too tired. 'We've only fought the Russians once in all our climacterics, in 1853, otherwise they've always been on our side. The British people must never forget that. The Russians have a marvellous sense of humour, like us...' etc. This record plays sometimes three times in one meal. I suppose it's better than 'When's Heather coming back?' or even 'I can't stand that dog.' He came to the Holy Communion service yesterday soon after saying: 'I don't go to church any more now.' But it was long and he stalked out before the end to go back to the television, and one couldn't blame him. He read a passage from St Paul very well, as he used to do at Brampton back in the 1950s.

Sunday 30th August

The last week has built up to a crescendo of activity ending with yesterday's courtyard fair. On Friday, which was hot, we got busy with signposting, visits from flower arrangers and stallholders and clearing the stables – which were choked with furniture, broken wooden beams, hay bales and dust – ready for scone teas and a display of water colours.

On Saturday the sky was overcast and so was my father. At breakfast he said he wasn't feeling well and would probably go to Scott's nursery at Merriott to buy a shrub. I got frosty because during the last few days he had accepted the fair as a necessary, if undesirable, community event. I said he would have to be there at 2 p.m. and stay for at least half an hour, one reason being that friends might turn up to see him. We had already been through the conversation at least twice daily: he was to spend half the afternoon in the Orangery, the other half in the library with guided tours coming occasionally up to the Charles II Dutch chair he (Victor Rex) sat in. Obviously he, or his sub-conscious, reckoned this was a poor deal because he was off towards Merriott well before 2. How far he got we never knew, but it was quite likely he would lose the way.

An hour and a half later I happened to meet the Range Rover coming down the drive, ready to plough into platoons of fair-goers outside the front door. I had car parking on my mind – the signing was inadequate and a lot of cars had missed the field and poured down the drive. I managed to turn him back to the tennis court and saw him off scowling, down to the Orangery – he had not come home with any new shrubs. One or two friends tracked him down there and later in the library. One man, Campbell Voullaire from Porlock, then totally unknown to us, came out cheerfully, saying he was unused to being offered so much alcohol at that time of day. Meanwhile Caroline was steering house tours round him as he staggered slightly through the hall. At one point she managed to nudge him and the bottle into the gramophone room just in time to allow the group to pass.

The fair was fun – I thought. The bouncy castle, thanks to Luke and Mima, stayed blown up and made a profit, as did pcs, darts, skittles and air rifles. The Bournemouth Bumpers danced and the ponies and carts looked bright and smart. The flowers in the church were of high quality, courtesy of North Poorton.

With the evening my father became more admiring about the fair, and less clear as to what it was. 'I think you're marvellous what you've done, simply marvellous fête, I don't think I've ever seen anything like it.' Good training behind that. I asked if any friends had come to see him. He couldn't remember. 'Oh yes, of course, Alexander (Hood).'

The next morning he was even jollier – 'thank you for moving the Range Rover back from the tennis court.' But then: 'I cannot stand that retriever, I think I shall shoot it if it stays here, you will take it back to London when you leave, won't you?' Pathetic.

Luckily this was in Stephen Scott's presence, as he had come, not before time, to witness an 'enduring power of attorney'. I think Stephen now understands, after years of broadly following my father's view, how much 'enduring' actually goes on at Mapperton. He acknowledged it as he got into his car. 'You really have got a difficult situation here at times, haven't you?'

Tuesday 15th September

I'm only now able to say what happened yesterday – an extra day I stayed on so as to attend a Telethon meeting in Plymouth. I had expected to have a nice quiet day 'catching up with things'...but one shouldn't expect anything.

7.15 a.m. and bright sun, perfect for looking out of the window... only to find cattle all over the orchard! Not Higgins', not Puzey's... surely not Fooks'? Yes it is theirs, 25 mainly Hereford–Friesian crosses which had somehow wandered out of the big field and along the main road. Lovely long grass, low–hanging cherry and apple branches, nice young elms to chew and scratch on. Eventually at 9 a.m., after two phone calls, David Fooks came and we led them back, leaving cowpats and hoof marks on the grass. Oh well.

My father found me a little brusque at breakfast. It was not just the cattle but he is getting very careless with the honey. I tried to cram in washing up, mending a plate, phoning and doing jobs in Beaminster. I cashed £20 off him (he's proving a useful bank) and tore off in the Chevette. I dropped an article in at the vicarage, bought stamps and meat and paint for Dick, returned a video, delivered a thankyou pc from Higgy to Dr Hudson and got back just in time to miss helping Mike to remove the bridge over the ha-ha.

At lunch and dinner, the same rotating question came about the times we would leave and arrive.

- I thought you were leaving today?

- No, tomorrow, but I'll be back at the weekend.
  Caroline comes on Friday.

- With the children?

- No, they are coming with me.

- What today? Are they having half–term?

- No, they're coming with me on Friday.

- I thought you said you were leaving today?

These questions are asked at a furious rate and have to be given short, precise answers – good for speech therapy I suppose. I accept our movements are confusing. The temptation is to be more and not less truthful and to provide more detail, thus creating more permutations, e.g., 'Are you going to London today?' should receive the more accurate but baffling 'No, Plymouth', immediately doubling all the odds of getting it wrong. The easier answer is just the downright, lying, exasperated 'yes'. Such conversations are not occasional but continuous, unless one works hard to broach a new subject and keep it alive.

We had a visit from the Koch family who used to live at the Rectory, including Jean-Alice's mother over from the US. My father kindly showed them the pictures. He has been more open with visitors recently and has not muttered about not opening the house, which we are being required to do by the Capital Taxes Office anyway as a condition of tax exemption. He was quite friendly with a group of sixth formers who drove down from Hinchingbrooke in a minibus on Sunday, hearing how the old place was. Some members of the Powell family came in on Sunday too. At this rate we'll have no trouble opening for the 26 statutory days.

The funniest episode was the Beaminster Fire Brigade practice in the evening. We got bad marks for unchecked indoor hoses – one with a bad leak – and frayed outdoor ones rolled up back to front. Mark Greenham, the electrician, caused roars of laughter when a jet shot out of the frayed canvas up his armpit. But our hydrants and water supply got high ratings. My father, to whom I introduced the fire leader in the library when it was all over, was impressed by the 7–8 minutes guaranteed arrival time. The fire leader was less impressed by the solitary figure at one end of a large house, and the charred sections of the floorboards. But we passed the test and – if we can find them – I'm sure we'll put the fires out.

Sunday 4th October

Yesterday a fallow stag appeared suddenly 25 yards away on the lower ride of Home Wood, looking majestically (a cliché for stags) towards us. We had the new puppy, Louis, with us – on a short string so he wouldn't chase young pheasants, but he was incapable of spotting them anyway. The stag was unmoved by our arrival and turned calmly uphill to join his does. George Brown was envious when we told him because he'd been looking out for him for days.

We spent an hour in Home Wood with Richard Ashdown, looking at ways of extracting timber for firewood, and another hour with George today walking both sides of Holeacre to see the mess left after the thinnings. In some places branches and brambles have made the track almost impassable even for Louis.

It was a quiet weekend after a very busy week. On Monday, for instance, I took 70 from the Dorset Natural History Society round the house in four groups. During one tour I found the old tatty 'Please do not Disturb' notice on the library door. Thinking disingenuously that it might be a mistake I knocked, as I sometimes (but not always) do, and asked if he really intended not to be disturbed by the house tour; to which the answer was 'yes', so I returned to the group with a set smile as if nothing was wrong. Fair enough. When the other groups came, the library was mysteriously empty – perhaps he had really taken the hint or, much more likely, he had extended his tea to the Orangery.

I was again wrong-footed on the question of central heating. As early as 8 a.m. he was on the phone to Tolmans to say it wasn't working. I heard him just too late as I came down the stairs and Cecil was there with breakfast. It only took him minutes to tell us nothing had been turned on. I might not have discovered this anyway. But at the weekend I heard the same voice on the telephone and was down the stairs, three at a time, in time to stop him. I inquired gently 'Were you ringing Tolmans?' 'No, it was Mike. I only wanted to tell him the hot water was off.' And so it was, but why and how? It was my move, so I muttered something about Heather speaking to Mike and waited. Mike eventually came, and said someone had turned the timer to full-time, so the boiler had burned out before it could be refilled. What could he say to that? Answer: 'I haven't touched the switches. I don't know which ones they are anyway.' Pass.

In matters of electricity and physics I have never interfered even as far as offering to read the gauges or the weather. He still calculates the figures down to ten or more decimal points, using a small printer: C and I long ago took a decision not to question them or use them. But there are areas like this where I wrestle with myself not to present any challenge on what I regard as distinctly hostile territory. He himself retains the extraordinary politician's mastery of the air – usually thin air – demonstrating supreme confidence in everything and nothing, provoking the opposition like Don Quixote and the windmills, which is an image he himself used a lot in the House of Commons and at home. This does not however relieve one of the uncanny feeling that he may be right and on some occasions he does indeed turn out to be so. It is a pity that neither of us has respected the other even as far as to presume that the other is right.

We went down to Loscombe with him for drinks with the Andrewes today – the first time he has been out to a drinks party this year. He met a lot of old friends whom, he says, he 'couldn't put a face to' any more. Some faces do remain, but he sometimes confuses people, even members of the family who are staying in the house. After half an hour he was exhausted and wanted to be taken home, though when we took him away some of his friends protested that he was perfectly all right and we shouldn't have removed him. How little even close friends and family seem to understand.

At breakfast today I asked my father if he had the same views on the House of Lords as he had had in the 1960s, e.g. that it was dull and ineffective compared to the Lower House. I actually knew that he had modified these views and had recognised the experience of many members of the House of Lords to be a genuine asset to Parliament. But I wanted to hear him say so.

I wasn't altogether disappointed, because at least he saw the necessity of giving me an answer based on proper reflection, rather than his old off-the-cuff political reply. He quoted WS Gilbert to the effect that 'they were doing nothing in particular but they did it very well'. He said that I would enjoy it – a mixed compliment from him but I decided to accept it with grace – and when I asked if he thought it needed reform he said, 'Well, you can reform it.'

The boys and Jemima all stayed in London this weekend. The boys now hardly ever come at weekends and I miss them – and their help around the place – but I can't blame them because they're at the age when friends are essential to them. The shooting season is starting soon – the duck are already coming in and Nigel Brown and Francis

Fooks got a couple yesterday – and with it the heavy negotiation with the boys for dates that suit them. It's lucky I prefer walking.

Friday 16th October

Last night was the night when a near-hurricane swept the south of England and blew down trees and power lines and Shanklin Pier. We were lucky in West Dorset. I woke up at 6 and the gale was blowing so hard I couldn't sleep, so I waited till light and got up to patrol around the house and garden. One cherry tree in the orchard blew over, six panes were smashed in the conservatory roof and some slates came off the dovecote but worse things happen at sea (and they did). It will take a while to pick up all the branches and heavy boughs which have fallen down in the garden.

My father wanted to know why the *Daily Telegraph* hadn't come (the *Times* and *Sun* somehow managed it but carried no news of the storm), and wasn't satisfied with the answer that there were no trains because trees were blocking the tracks. We had Richard Olney, a RHMC researcher looking at Victorian manuscripts, who was stranded, and my father was very courteous about how he was going to leave, but without any solutions. Last night I went in to say it was time for supper and he said: 'I think I've already eaten, I don't want any more.' This has happened two or three times in the last fortnight, Shirley tells me. So Dr Olney and I went to work on ours and the extra steak, grateful for that but sorry that we would not be able to explore nineteenth century prime ministers with him or Baldwin's attitude to record-keeping – luckily for him perhaps. At lunch today it emerged that Louisa, 6th Countess of Sandwich, had grown up with Lady Castlereagh and had received a £3,000 jointure when her husband George died – a fortune in 1818 which must account for her furniture-buying in Paris, preparing for another half-century at Hinchingbrooke. She lived until 1862, some of the time abroad. We found a delightful letter to her from Carlyle on his travels in Scotland.

Confusion reigned all day about who was coming or going, or whether the trains were running or the roads were clear. It seemed to me better to keep out of the way, and neither ask questions nor give any definitive reply. But old men are persistent all right.

This weekend began with heavy rain which threatened to drown the shoot, but by lunchtime the sun was warming up the village hall where the guns assembled with their sandwiches and thermoses. My father had by then peered outside and decided to stay away. I went to Crewkerne to wait for 40 minutes for Jemima after her train had broken down in Salisbury. Later we had a harvest cum Halloween cum All Saints party in the hall, with a short speech by George saying farewell to the Fairalls, who are leaving Mapperton Farm in a week's time.

Sunday morning breakfast reminded me – imagining myself still young – of the heavy glue-like conversation of adults who stick together even when they are incompatible. How they try to deceive one another, pushing the polite exchanges back and forth in between quick glances; occasionally my father and I stare uncomprehending at each other and then fall back into the rhythm. Julia is staying and doing her best to lighten the atmosphere, but she gives my father too much credit and tries to explain the unexplainable; I think I gave up long ago. The Neubronners appear (from Bonn), pleased to be on time and expressing satisfaction with Mapperton solitude. Timmy aged 5 flies in looking for Frosties and parks himself next to his grandfather. No one eats the mackerel but it will wait for kedgeree.

Richard Ashdown is chopping wood; Caroline and I also go out with a power saw, and George loaded with pheasants bound for London comes down to find out what the noise is. How lucky we are to have such a reliable friend, watching over such a vast area. Mr Suddards has cut his hedge ruthlessly down to six feet though he only has one eye and his ladder is on a 45 degree slant. Mrs S won't do the church flowers, so Alice and Dick rally as always with their chrysanthemums and I put some autumn sprays in a high vase, ready for Evensong.

I tried to get him to attend, but the battle was obviously a losing one and I settled for a brief appearance *'pour encourager les autres'*. not thinking at the time how ambiguous the phrase was. But he reneged again, saying he was in the wrong clothes. I pointed out he would have to change into a dinner jacket anyway, so why not a suit? He agreed but minutes later I caught him in the passage: 'I don't think I'll come this evening', so I gave up. At 6.15 a few back pews were filling up and I helped Chris Koch to light the candles. Then at 6.30 sharp I happened to glance into the muniment room, down the steps from the choir, and there he was with his half-finished vodka, looking at his watch. Earlier, I had asked if he would like to hear the music of the harmonium and he had said he could just as well hear church music on the radio. Now there he was, sitting by the church door as though he was at a concert. I got Chris to wave at him and went back satisfied.

It was a magnificent choral evensong starting with a Gloria and ending with a Jubilate, sung by about 15 Beaminster choristers. Old Mrs Cox, whose husband Ralph at Marsh Farm was the organist here for years, came with her niece, and several from Melplash. Chris reminded us we could all be saints even if we were only timing eggs – of all images to choose. Caroline read a bit of Jeremiah about the new covenant enabling us all to start again (yet again). Luke – practising for his driving test – and Jemima – muddled – stayed well away which I tried not to be sorry about.

The end of the evening came during ITV news (fascinating item about the retiring Chinese old guard) when there was a crash on the floor of my father's bedroom. I hare up the stairs to find him stark naked on the floor by his chair, unable to get up. 'thank goodness you came, how did you know?'

I heaved him up and straightened his clothes on the chair; he seemed to be unhurt but tottered again as he climbed into pyjamas and then exhausted into bed. What else can one expect when the drinks begin after breakfast. But *que faire?*

Monday 2ⁿᵈ November

He seems to have forgotten completely that he fell down last night, and I wonder how often he remembers that he has fallen, let alone to tell anyone afterwards.

Tuesday 3ʳᵈ November

Yesterday I visited Marsh Farm to see the site of a proposed feeder, a wooden cupboard 17 feet high which enables intake of concentrated feed to be measured by computer – surely Mapperton's arrival in the space age.

'Are you visiting all the farms, Johnny?' (all four of them). 'That's good. I used to go round all the tenants. Do you remember we had that Willys jeep?' (I do, but the Range Rover's quite exciting, isn't it, stroking the stone walls on the way into Beaminster.) 'I don't get out so much now.' (Oh no, what about driving your more pliable guests off to Abbotsbury or Portland? And you seem to go off to Bridport at the drop of a hat, for a tired piece of plaice or a haircut.)

We drove round Bridport garden centres and stores yesterday looking for goldfish, to replace four Japanese ones allegedly stolen by the heron 'from the coast'. The plastic owl is back in place after the hurricane a fortnight ago, but obviously isn't an adequate deterrent. 'I don't know where to find little fishes – do you think Harrods would have them?' I don't know but Clapham Aquatics might if you're prepared to pay 60p for them. You can get some with black spines and fluffy tails if you look carefully.

The disaster news this week is the imminent closure of Pines, Beaminster's Fortnum and Mason. 'Oh dear, what shall we do now?' He was genuinely perplexed when he opened the letter. Anyone who has become used to the click of the back door on Friday afternoons when the standard order has arrived in a cardboard box, perhaps over 25 years, must feel it like a bombshell. But a Bridport grocer is being investigated.

His hands, cut by various falls, seem to be healing at last and we have actually cancelled a doctor's appointment. I got him to show them to Shirley in the kitchen. 'Oh, does she know about that sort of thing?' (Oh no, she's only the only woman living in your house the entire week.)

Sunday 8ᵗʰ November

A brave pheasant wandered out on to the main road beyond Marsh Farm this morning I met him on the bend at Storridge – just the place for a suicide mission – as I was bringing up the Sunday papers. This weekend my father met his first great grandchild, Toni's daughter Elena. They posed together for photographs and it was difficult to tell who was enjoying it most. This was also the weekend that Anne stayed, and we managed to get Hinch's approval for a new loo in the gramophone room after a lot of heart–searching. Why can't people sit in comfort in the same room as they are playing gramophone records? In country houses there has always been a happy harmony of loos and shooting gear or golf clubs – why not music? Obviously it is a territorial problem for my father but as there is a basin in there anyway, already in use, he won't notice it after a few weeks.

> *CAROLINE ADDS: Well, it was nothing to do with country house harmony, or eccentricity or golf clubs, or even John's father. The previous Christmas we had my mother in a wheelchair staying and John's a bit doddery aunt Betts. It was a trial for both of them. On the ground floor there was only a commode in the "boot room" beside the broom cupboard, behind an oak screen tastefully placed there by me. So when either wanted the loo, off we rushed or trundled to the boot room, to find the commode. The boot room was also close to a couple of stairs down which Betts could have fallen and my mother's wheelchair slipped. After this daily obstacle race, I resolved I would never allow two elderly women not to be able to reach a loo. My father in law's selfishness, "I don't want a loo in there", didn't harden my resolve. It didn't have to; it merely confirmed my irritation at his selfishness.*

Advent Sunday. My father suddenly said at breakfast that he was going to stop doing the weather – in fact he said he had stopped. I could hardly believe it, partly because it has been so much part of his daily routine, partly because his amnesia made me wonder if he could remember to stop. We shall see.

It is the culmination of several days of drama. On Tuesday he had another heavy fall, and cut himself again and left a trail of blood. Shirley and Stan couldn't trace exactly where he had fallen, somewhere between the hall and the bathroom. Then the day after, he fell again, this time when he was in the library, half in earshot, and they lifted him up and helped him into bed. I rang up and heard about it and so came rapidly down, expecting the worst, and arrived to find complete calm – he had even decided to drive off to the dentist in Bridport as though nothing had happened.

I decided to have a three point plan: driving, drinking and helping. Somehow we have got to persuade him to stop driving, because he is as much a risk to others as to himself. If he cuts down his drinking to only one glass of anything per day, there's some chance he will be able to stagger up to bed. We need to step up the support system, too, because Shirley cannot turn herself into a night nurse. It may be time for agency nursing. It is certainly time for doctors' letters.

In the office on Friday there was a deceptive air of organisation when suddenly there was a power cut, the boiler stopped and the heating went off. After umpteen phone calls to plumbers and electricians all day, Mr Hallett came up and diagnosed faulty wiring and mended it. Meanwhile I had given myself a useful fuse box lesson and mended two doubtful fuses: the labelling of circuits is appalling. Comically the Orangery lights decided to go on for two nights running and my father was convinced it was a practical joke. 'There must be someone down there, I don't know how they could have got in.' Answer, because you've lost a key and the side door is open. In fact I think it has to do with his time switch. Tolmans have been up twice recently to find the switches were set wrong.

Saturday was an excellent shooting day for Luke and those who took part. I was a bit miffed not to be able to walk with them, knowing that so many things might go wrong down at the house. I walked up the hill with Serena Scott—Thomas (staying for the weekend with Tom Oates) and watched the pheasants winging their way round the hill to avoid the guns. My father still kindly asks guests, and even the boys and me, whether they would like to use one of his guns. 'I don't go shooting any more now, you take my gun,' he says as though he had only just made the decision. It rebounds on the boys sometimes when they are made to feel like intruders, borrowing guns they have been using for years. This makes me fulminate at the selfishness of his situation, the way in which he can sit on the family possessions like some great octopus, preventing anyone from getting near. 'I'll have the woodcock,' he said last night at dinner. There was only the one. Was it greed, or envy of other people shooting, or just an owner's statement? There are so many underground thoughts in people's minds that it is sometimes wrong to summarise them. There are certainly plenty of them in mine at this moment.

I have been planning a speech for the Pepys Club on Tuesday on the theme of 'Pepys in Africa' – prompted by the fact that the guest speaker, Peter Pilkington, the High Master of St Paul's, used to teach in Africa. It's a bit of a cheat because Pepys got no further than Tangier, supervising the destruction of the garrison against the Moors in 1683. But he had his fair share of mosquitoes and fury with colonial mismanagement.

My father said: 'Have you done any research? I used to do a lot of research. When are you speaking? Next month. Tuesday? Good gracious. How will you manage it?' I have no idea. I also have a little work to do of my own, but you wouldn't know about that. Yes, I left Christian Aid (mainly to come and help here). No, I don't go to Hinchingbrooke to lecture, sorry yes I do if that will stop you asking the same questions about it.

I came down two days early because I knew that the doctors would deliver a letter today which might change the course of history.

The letter, strongly urging my father to surrender his driving licence because he was no longer medically fit to drive, duly arrived this morning by hand. He muttered about it twice before opening it after breakfast, thinking it to be a bill. I let him carry it into the library where it quickly landed in the waste paper basket. On his way out – to drive the Range Rover – I asked him about it and he immediately complained that there was no reason for him to stop driving.

I reminded him then and again at lunch that he had had several falls, that his circulation wasn't good, that he had alcohol problems and that the writing was on the wall. Typically, he rallied at the thought of everyone combining against him – doctors, family, solicitor this time instead of other MPs as in the past – and behaved like a fox underground, saying he would go to court and get the judge's opinion if necessary. I pointed out that the law was clear and the decision had already been taken

He decided the weather was too foul to go out in so I got a lift from Bob Gilbert over to Manor Farm, North Poorton, where I wanted to look at the new drainage system. Bob showed me where new pipes had been laid to pump the water uphill to a tank. Alan Fooks took me round the farm, pointing out missing tiles and thatch which had had its day. Then I walked over to Betty Fooks, Wilf's widow, who gave me a cup of tea in her very spruce bungalow. I could hardly believe she was the mother of four stalwart brothers running the farm – she seemed so young and petite. She told me she had grown up at Burcombe and had married the boy next door. She remembered my grandfather walking from Copse Barn to Mapperton in the 1950s: he used to wear a Panama which her father rather envied, and the funny thing was that he never walked back. Presumably Mrs Labouchere took him back in her elegant car, discussing her garden which was then only 25 years old: people still remembered the party given for London designers to come down and see it. But it was a long walk from Copse Barn. Perhaps he took a mug of cider off the Fooks' on the way down: the postman used to have 7 or 8 at lunchtime, according to Alan, and went off with a very red face.

I walked back over the stream and up through the wood to Coltleigh, passing a spinney of Christmas trees. A Bridport firm has ordered a 25-footer from us but I think the extraction will be too costly. No answer from my knock on George Brown's door, so I continue over the hill past the bungalow. In the half dark the eight Jacob's sheep watched me walk down to the house – the woolly one still looking like an Edward Lear creation.

That evening I avoided the driving issue and had a hot bath before driving down to Victor Crutchley's Zambia talk at the Friends Meeting house in Bridport – and a nice beery evening at the George afterwards.

Friday 4th December

My father takes an hour to get up for breakfast, partly because of the cuts on his hands. Somehow we all stand around waiting for him, unable to help. His voice has dropped an octave, I notice, and – after a lot of clearing of throat – sounds more vigorous before breakfast, as though to compensate for the rest of the day. I do the papers and he is ready. The battle is joined at breakfast again, with him in fine fighting form. Eventually he tries to shut me up and I say, sorry, you're up against me over this and I tried to explain the decision was already made. He won't be budged so we'll have to let the insurance company do it. After that, if necessary, it'll be the police. It's sad, of course, but too bad. My parting shot was sincerely felt: I simply have no more time to waste on it.

Thursday 17th December

The last ten days have sadly seen a sudden deterioration in my father's health. After the weekend Kate came down with George Lansdowne and spent an evening with him, reporting that he was quite shaky though happily sharing memories with George – perhaps the last of his friends to see him on his old form. I was in London.

Kate said that after supper he was either drunk or sickening and broke off early to go to bed. I concluded the former. But the next night he was found by Heather shivering in the bath with the water run out, unable to get out until Stan and Shirley came to help. By then meals had become so erratic that we had all had trouble in predicting his movements, normally so punctual that we have seen him as a sort of house clock. We have had to use a 'kiddi call' radio so that at least he can be heard getting out of bed in time for us to help him.

Now all this, too, has changed because he has been found to have caught pneumonia. Obviously he has gradually become vulnerable through general frailty and undernourishment, and who knows whether the draughts in the house or the 'cold bath' tipped the balance. For some time I have had the feeling that some drastic event was imminent, but thought it would be more likely to be a heavy fall. He has been so self-sufficient in the last 20 years that, strangely, there is no cause for regret that this has happened: it had to come, and perversely there is even the feeling of relief that it has come, although the event brings with it a whole new bag of difficulties.

Help has since arrived in the usual form – doctors, nurses, friends and family coming and going, and I see no point in recording everyone who arrived and when, those who visited and others who just telephoned. We have followed the principle that he would prefer to be helped in his own home, with familiar things around him. But the job has been far from easy for the helpers and we have been considering for the first time whether he himself might be more comfortable elsewhere, without any special place in mind but just in case we have to make a sudden decision.

Since his temperature came down he has been propped up on pillows and unwilling to get out of bed, which is our major problem. He has had sudden hallucinations which we put down to alcohol withdrawal: a fountain at the end of the bed, a group of young people in the corner of his room. He mutters composite replies full of old thoughts and tailing off into embarrassment. I've tried to read him Christmas cards and found myself inventing things to say when there was nothing, protecting him unnecessarily from the outside world. He comes alive when outsiders appear. What he really needs, as always, is the stimulus of those who are prepared to challenge him and humour him – I have never willingly been among them and am therefore not the best nurse, although of course we have a lot to talk about provided he can talk. When visitors come – like Stephen Scott who called after shooting on Saturday – I try to create a tea and lemon party or a glass of sherry, to provide a sense of occasion although he can now hardly drink a glass down.

His driving licence and insurance have been cancelled, which now seems hardly worth recording in spite of the battles we have had. It is hard to judge whether this blow had properly sunk in before his illness, but it must have contributed to the downward trend in his morale. But again, it was inevitable.

On Sunday I had to return to London to work, while Caroline stayed to man the decks with the Clarks, Heather and various agency nurses backing her up. For the last four days they have been up and down stairs, helping him to the bathroom or the commode, spoon feeding him and chatting away to keep him alert. What a struggle, though. He lies there with his eyes closed; nodding off to sleep until someone necessarily disturbs him. On the whole he requires nothing and answers to no one – except the call of the bladder.

Tuesday 22nd December

It's impossible to predict whether my father will recover or if he does what form his life will take. The Dutch burgomaster's chair given to Charles II has been removed for repair and it is hard to imagine him sitting in it again, lifting his port glass and nodding in front of the television, oblivious of the world like some Victorian mechanical toy. Such has been the strength of his personality that these images fade very slowly. I have been slow to realise, even with Caroline's help, how exaggerated this impact has been on me and on the rest of the family, and how artificial is the awesome sense of standing in the staircase hall before going in to see him. Mrs Labouchere, Mapperton's last owner, spent a long time bed-ridden above that hall, vowing to reopen the window looking over it which had been walled up. Who can say whether my father, too, on the opposite landing of the old Tudor wing, may not reign up there for months to come, served by a line of faithful helpers ministering to his every unexpressed wish? Usually the helpers, like Mrs L's butler, take over the cellar first. In any case I won't be one of them: my time would be up first.

I am sitting writing this in the library, in the only peaceful corner of the house, listening to Berlioz' *L'Enfance du Christ*. Shirley and I tried to help my father into bed this morning after the nurse left, but he collapsed on to the floor. He has tired himself out with the physiotherapist, sparkling as she is, like his tonic and lemon. George Martelli, a very old friend, also dropped in for a rather doleful glass of sherry. My father's conversation is limited but I find I am fascinated by the random thoughts in his head – perhaps because they contain secrets, but they are also colourful and strangely put together. For example, he said something like: 'We will have to make a presentiment to Parliament to enable me to be conveyed around the country' – possibly a reference to losing the freedom to drive. Then he said he had a row with someone in the House and the other chap afterwards sent him round the fine leather waistcoat he wears, as a goodwill gesture. He is continually making plans to go downstairs, to the dining–room or even to catch a train. His mind has sadly wandered further astray since his illness, and yet at certain times he still behaves like the captain.

Christmas Day

A day I have been dreading, because of the impossibility of satisfying demand, but looking back on it I think we have done quite well. Everyone either watched the television, attended the morning service, ate more than adequately and enjoyed themselves in spite of an impossible timetable, and we were even relaxed enough to play a family game after dinner by the fire after all the presents had been opened. What a model Christmas!

We thought of bringing my father downstairs for a brief appearance – Dr Hudson's idea, but it didn't appeal either to my father or to Luke who was to help me with the fireman's lift. I am not sure I wholly trust those stair-rails either – it might have been a terrible end for all three of us.

Tuesday 29th December

Christmas isn't over yet: 50 people come in for a sherry and a quick sight of my father before lunch. Visitors produce from him a smile and a lit-up face, genuinely pleased to see them if he recognises them – but like the physiotherapist they also tire him out, so he lies for most of the day with his eyes closed, even when we try to pour soup and Complan into him. Solid food is now very limited, but last night I succeeded in giving him some delicious Weetabix and milk and honey. Caroline had to stay up late to collect Luke from a party in Dorchester; I picked up Orlando and a friend from the Half Moon and then had to get up at 6.45 a.m. to deliver them to Maiden Newton station. Meanwhile Julia has come back, and was very tearful, thinking about the hard decision we face, whether to get him proper nursing in hospital, or to allow him – as the phrase goes – to have a peaceful end at home.

Thursday 31st December

New Year's Eve, and the day we had finally decided to move my father into hospital in Dorchester. There is no pretending that the decision is solely on health grounds – everyone around him has deserved a break from the exhausting Christmas routine and we shall all benefit from a 'few days off' – a euphemism, as it turned out, for nearly a fortnight. Dr Hudson arrived before 8 and we all had a cup of tea, trying to avoid being the clutch of anxious relations outside the door. 'Hinch, we are going to move you to hospital to help you to get better', or some such wording which he was bound not to hear or listen to. I was however relieved that he 'seemed' to go along with it – there are so many shades of misunderstanding on both sides, and of pretence on ours, that it is hard to feel any positive emotions, or those which go in any direction.

The ambulance was long delayed and we eventually gave up staring out of the window. In fact there was little to suggest a Chekhovian drama. The sun shone and Richard Ashdown started bringing logs into the front gate just as the ambulance arrived. Two tough guys went upstairs with the doctor and Janet the nurse, but minutes later Janet came out and said, 'We've got a problem – he doesn't want to go', and I had visions of the scene which I had half dreaded, half expected for ages, a sort of filmed Victorian melodrama of which I felt this would be the final act, featuring VR printed on the letter box at the top of the drive, and scenes of my father's birth in Bruton Street and straw laid down in the mews, only five years after the old Queen died. In the event I repeated what the doctor had said early in the morning and we persuaded him to be carried down, wrapped in blankets with his hat on to keep off the wind. He was swung quite energetically into the ambulance – I suppose they must know what they are doing – and all of us, including Julia and Timmy, waved him off.

1988

Tuesday 11th January

Ten days later, after expert treatment at the Winterbourne Hospital, it is just possible to say that he is better: his cuts have healed up, his conversation is a bit clearer and he must be as comfortable as he will ever be. His appetite is still the major problem. I come into the hospital hopeful that the nursing staff have succeeded in feeding him better but they have failed just as we did. My mother says he should be left and not forced to eat, and when I mentioned this to him yesterday he said, 'she's quite right, as she is about everything else'. He must be exasperated when relations begin to act like nurses and talk in baby language about eating a little bit more, just one more bite, etc. And yet I challenge anyone to live alongside another person and not try to give them every possible chance to stay alive. The difficulty comes in knowing what his own feelings are and whether they are relevant. I can't help being amused by his diversionary tactics, the normal ones being to push the food away (even spit it out) because 'I don't feel like it' or 'I've already eaten'.

More serious even is the state of his mind, but I don't think it is any worse than at Christmas. I find I can keep up a thread of conversation for several minutes, and amnesia only sets in when you allow him to wander – though it is tiring. I had a lucid conversation yesterday about the future of the Range Rover, which seems doomed, and he recognised that Mrs Clark would not want to drive him around in it and that we must get something more practical which would actually fit into the Dorset lanes instead of alarming everyone for miles around. His bank manager, with an eye to overdraft, reminds us that the number plate VM I is now much more valuable than the car, and with the level of nursing going on they'll both be used up.

Caroline has just phoned from London to say that he has telephoned her to say he is in hospital in Dorchester and hopes to come out tomorrow. He must be – could he be? – on the mend? It seems most unlikely.

Tuesday 18th January

Four days home, and – amazing to report – he is actually picking up again. Not eating properly, but taking more in, talking more normally and walking more steadily. Most of this is the effect of two weeks' careful nursing in Dorchester, but Rebecca, our new Tasmanian nurse (from, of all places, Montagu) is expert at getting him up and downstairs. His convalescent demands are beginning to make us groan like the old times. Can't I go into the dining room, Could I have two hot water bottles, Would you (i.e. me) like a cocktail, What time is it? His gimlet eye takes in everything that is going on and often catches me picking up something: what are you taking, what's that, is that my spectacle case (no it's the TV control). He is still very confused about life and repeats things the whole time but one can tolerate that more knowing that he has, despite all expectation, pulled back considerably from the brink.

We were nearly over the top last night when he said he felt unwell in the library at around 8 p.m. (the heating, maybe, on top of a glass of wine) so I manoeuvred him to the stairs and he started sagging and losing breath rapidly. This is it, I told myself and felt suddenly inert myself, but called out to Becky who was upstairs and she rushed the wheelchair towards us. We got him into it and she asked him firmly to breathe in and soon he came out of his faint and asked unexpectedly where the children were. She calls him Hinch which I find strange, but if you think about it any nurse is on very intimate terms from the word go and has to speak to him like a child sometimes – she herself is all of 21.

Meanwhile life goes on as normally as possible. This morning George Brown and I went to Parnham to discuss deer control with Chris Sadd, the forester at Hooke employed by John Makepeace. It was very productive and I learned a lot, including the fact that roe deer tend to stay in one area whereas fallow cover many miles and therefore must be controlled co-operatively. The forest has been thinned out and more deer are coming in, so they are creating special areas for them to browse away from young plantations. There are poachers and 'freelance' stalkers about, so we are going to organise a bigger meeting for owners and stalkers over a 5 mile radius, to be held at Mapperton in early March.

The garden looks quite neat under Mr K's single-handed care, but the foul if warm weather has kept me indoors, except for short walks with Louis the labrador puppy. Today we had to clear the whole drawing room to prepare for sanding and polishing tomorrow. Shirley had the bright idea of shunting books along in the wheelchair, but I found I was distracted by my grandmother's diary c 1900 and a little red leather volume surprisingly inscribed 'Earl of Sandwich – Postmaster General'. We then had tea visitors – the Powells and Joyce – to see my father, followed by a new vicar, Richard Thornburgh, who is interested in mystery plays and so may well get roped into the Courtyard Fair committee. He helped me to dig deep into Julia's enormous Christmas cake which, to my shame, has been abandoned in a cupboard. We must try and clear it before she comes back on Thursday.

Caroline and I are rather divided – we can't really afford financially to be in the same place. Neither of us is really doing enough work of our own and we will have to dig into some heirloom soon to keep afloat. I suppose we are lucky to be able to do this, but I don't seem to shake off the feeling that living is artificial unless one lives off earned income. I expect I'll grow out of this sometime.

A nice letter has come to my father from Lord Kennet, whom he must have been kind to as a young naval officer in Portland years ago. I have acknowledged it, and rather hope he will come down and stay so we can get an inside view of the appalling SDP/Liberal struggles.

Friday 12th February

These words of wisdom are better put down the same day. I find too often I try to write them out from notes in trains or London buses and then can't get them in the right order. But today is genuinely today.

I came down yesterday to find the New Zealand nurse, Kathy, had settled in well and had had 24 hours overlap with Becky who is off on European travels. It's now a month since my father left hospital and he has picked up a lot. With a bit of prompting he rang Anne up to wish her a happy birthday and obviously impressed her, though she would have liked a fraction more spontaneity.

His timetable with nurses is more erratic when we are down: I think he sees me as a potential drinking companion (ultimately *manqué*) rather than a son:

'Is there any more we can put in that glass?' (note the 'we')

'Well, you had one for supper and the nurse said...' (I retreat)

'Nurse, whose nurse?'

'You've had a nurse since you came out of hospital.'

'Have I? Oh that nice girl? When was I in hospital?' and so on.

I've got to get hold of a fleece to replace the ripple mattress, the airbed hired from Borehamwood. I thought the Fooks' might produce one but of course it would be uncured – they have given me two addresses. Otherwise there's always my tatty old Hungarian sheepskin, if I cut the pockets off, or even the black bear with claws covering the chaise longue in the library – provided they don't scratch him in the night.

It has been one of those bright clear cold days with 20-mile views. I thought he would like to go out for the first time so we drove down to Beaminster square with Kathy. The Midland Bank girls sent 'regards to Mr Montagu' as I cashed his cheque for Mr Kennedy. The Bugler's petrol pump attendant chatted to him through the window. We gazed up at Lewesdon Hill, looked at Pines' empty window and the new car park and then drove back home before he could say it was all too much – which it evidently was from his behaviour at lunch. He has this ghastly habit of pushing back his chair if people are not talking to him and gesturing for help, before he has even finished a course. Meals last about five minutes, so not surprisingly all but the nurse opt out of the other meals which he usually has on a tray. I find I am trying to encourage him to eat in the dining–room when he would much rather not. I suppose it's because I would prefer him to go back to 'his old life' rather than lead a 'non–life' – but perhaps it's only me who looks for stimulation which is just not there any more. Perhaps he should just carry on off-stage. I could read to him the lines '... this petty pace from day to day' and see if he catches on. I looked at him meaningfully this afternoon and said 'How's life?' and he said, as always, 'so–so', as though there was a helpless understanding that there was not much in it, nor any will to find any.

Meanwhile the garden is suddenly alive with Copp's men rebuilding stone walls – one dry wall propping up the iceberg rose bed, one pillar split by cotoneaster, another wall crumbling behind an old cement seat, and a fast subsiding flight of steep steps above the pool. Another month and the garden is open again. The County Council have failed us with sign-posting for the second year running. Deer have chewed off the tops of wallflowers and rosebuds, and all I can do is write about it in the parish magazine in the new 'Mapperton has come alive again' column. Oh well, the sun has got his hat off and it's the shoot dinner tomorrow night, so things must be all right, eh, what do you say Wurzel? (He doesn't.)

I must remember not to leave the cat under the microwave detector tonight where he could set off the alarm – though it never moves once he's asleep. I find I am imagining conversations. 'That cat, whose is it?' shudders Higgy's ghost, half threatening, half afraid. 'Before you ask,'

I reply, 'the black dog is called Louis and is Orlando's. You used to have dogs, too. Remember you once gave me a labrador just like him?'

Thursday 18th February

I have been having breakfast with Kathy, the New Zealand nurse, in the dining–room but have noticed social incongruities which leave me uncomfortable. If the male nurse from Yeovil had been here, he would have been happier eating in the kitchen chatting to Shirley; and I would have accepted that. But what if she had been a female nurse from Yeovil or London – would I have felt the same? Doubtful. Do I simply prefer female NZ company – no, I don't believe it's that. Perhaps the best course is for me to eat in the kitchen and save the extra bother. But I enjoy 'the old breakfast' too much for that.

Out in the back yard I found no less than five of Copp's men eating sandwiches on the back of the trailer in the garage, keeping out of the wind. The new wall along the field looks handsome. I walked round with Gary Copp looking at various rebuilding works – I hope the bill for these stays away until rents come in April, but they look very nice. Hidden in the St John's wort, above the crumbling grotto by the pool where my father kept peacocks, I spotted a stone seat I had never seen. Maddeningly, Caroline already knows about it.

Richard Ollard came for the day and looked through the 1st Earl's journals. I enjoy his company and have high hopes he might propose something to his publishers, HarperCollins, though he has promised himself no more 17th century biographies. I then worked on the final page proofs of my Africa report for Save the Children.

In the afternoon Kathy was off, so I drove Higgy up the hill to Hooke. I asked him about childhood memories but he could only grunt, 'Awful lot of cars in there'. We gazed at shimmering light on the sea beyond Bridport and came back for lemon curd sandwiches. Stephen Scott arrived later with documents about the power of attorney, which we are now registering, not before time. He read through the document and seemed to understand it.

I managed to break the last nice sherry glass, symbolically maybe, but Stephen was kind enough to say I made at least as good a vodka martini as my father.

Friday 19th February

This morning I went into my father's bedroom to hear yells of protest. He was attempting to sit up in bed with firm but gentle instructions from Kathy to lean forward, despite obvious back pains. 'But I don't want to get out of bed, I want to get back into the bed,' he glared at both of us, looking exactly like the Sixties Vicky cartoons of him standing furiously over his motley political crew, the frustrated admiral who, like Captain Haddock, gives pleasure to millions but is not ultimately able to alter the course of the ship. If this is unfair I will submit to reading all the press cuttings again and revise my opinion. I plead guilty to getting at him when he is down, but then I have only had the full perspective in the last five years since we've been here. In truth, I have only recently felt able to think about his life objectively, without all the psychological intrusion of our relationship. Politically I am sure we were not always on opposite sides, because after the war he favoured social reforms and good relations with Africa. His social background, much more than mine, moulded his attitudes which only crystallised in his late Fifties when he turned into his own cartoon. This means I still have ten years, if I follow anything like this pattern of maturity. I shall need rather more, the way things are going.

Sunday 28th February

There are two more Jacobs lambs in the Rectory orchard today, keeping just ahead of the daffodils. They have very little grass left, so we have decided to move them on to the hill and to fence the top half of the orchard beyond the tennis court, as extra grazing for them. But this year the new ram we borrowed seems much less productive than Mohammed Ali, and he is a Dorset Down, so we'll sell the lambs and start again with a Jacob's ram.

My father has had no less than three temporary nurses this weekend and has been nice to them all, without telling them apart. 'My dear, you must have many better things to do than to look after me.' 'Not yet,' smiled the one from Maiden Newton, eyeing him in bed one morning. For most of the day he sits in the library, gazing unselectively at the TV screen, watching sometimes TV news, sometimes highly unsuitable even violent programmes until you realise that he will watch anything. This doesn't, somehow, convince one to leave him alone: I am forever trying to get him to watch 'suitable' TV as though he were a child, with the same mindless optimism as a parent has.

Tuesday 8th March

Surely the first day of spring. Last night the sunset beamed a brilliant golden strip of light across the whole garden, lighting up the red willows and copses just visible from the house. This morning was cloudy but warm, and the daffodils are coming out rapidly to join the primroses and crocuses down the drive and around the grass circle in front of the house.

Bad news: a lamb has fallen into a hole in the orchard and died. Mike mutters about the lack of pasture but the real cause is excavation for drainage below the Old Rectory stable that should have been filled in. The Jacob's sheep have all been moved to the opposite field, at any rate, waiting for their new orchard.

My father was mightily confused today, something to do with some money he thought he had received and should pay into the bank. We all get infected and scramble round him looking for an imaginary cheque. He turns every little cheque stub and loose item in his wallet over and over. Kathy the nurse and I stare at each other, in exasperation and amusement; she tells me he has several times talked about going down to the bank and taking off in the Range

Rover (now in a Bayswater garage awaiting sale), and she has had to contradict him. He doesn't mention the car to me but asks: 'Have you been down to the bank in the square, Johnny, you know, up the three steps, is it?' I reassure him one of us has been in every week. In the end, after most of a lunch on the subject, I manage to steer him off. It wouldn't do at all to encourage this train of thought: to think that he might even want to start keeping accounts and reading the electricity meter again...

I left him for the usual hour or so after lunch, looking in on him once, then I suddenly heard the ping of his telephone. I was just asking Stan if Julie, his daughter, could have been using it when it dawned on me. Then the other phone rang and Mike Caplen said: 'Your father's just rung to say his fire's gone out.' I roared with laughter and felt pleased that, although he had stolen a march on me, he was obviously capable of getting an urgent message out. I went in and made up the fire: he was sitting calmly in his chair watching TV.

Another sign of spring: Jeff Truscott is back and pruning away in the orchard. I went to say hello and we chatted, but when I passed on Caroline's message about the two honeysuckles being pruned he seemed less than enthusiastic. Later he rightly pointed out we have no tools for the mowers, all of which appear to have packed up, anticipating the season.

We had an important meeting last night with local stalkers and landowners to discuss deer numbers and culling policy. Shirley stood by with coffee but they all wanted cider or beer. As a consultation it was highly successful and we decided to hold a census of the fallow around the rut in October. On Sunday stalking and on the merits of sika deer, we agreed to differ.

The office desk, as I write, is piled high with paperwork, much of it routine work for my father on top of the usual office business. I could sit here for hours and probably should, just writing letters and paying bills. I also have a UN meeting on Africa to address in Bridport tomorrow night, and haven't prepared for it; for some reason I feel no anxiety about it.

This evening I dropped in on Joyce and Alf. It sounds as if the stories of the lamb and my father's fire have been all round the village. Alf and I chat about Dick helping with the church porch decoration – Alf is going to hold ladders and generally stick around. 'E's 82, mind, 'e didn't ought a go up ladders.' Joyce has walked up to the milk churns <u>and</u> cleaned the car. 'The winders was all dirty when we went to Yeovil so I washed and polished 'e off.' They told how they wickedly tease their next door neighbours, the Larkins, by saying I'd just been in and had said I'd do up the house for them. Poor Jimmy and Joe, so polite they won't ask for a door for the garden shed, let alone landlord's obligations. Alf will look out for things they really need.

Sunday 28th March

March has proved a very different story. Instead of watching gradual progress, we have seen gradual decline since the middle of the month. He was suddenly much weaker just as Kathy was starting to take her holiday, and she had difficulty getting him upstairs. Then came an Austrian nurse called Mrs T, with a strong personality, who became known as the dragon. One of her famous comments was 'this is not a country house, this is filthy'. We all stuck it for ten days until yesterday, when I decided to fire the dragon. She had tried to organise the whole household and nearly caused mass resignations. Someone whispered, 'she'll either kill or cure him' and she overheard. After the storm which followed, I decided it was best for all of us if she left. Medically, it was a good thing to have had a casualty nurse that week; anything might have happened and he was getting the occasional blackout. Besides this, his heel was bad and his sores had returned and needed regular dressing. We have been nursing 24 hours, with Shirley, Caro and I providing extra help to give temporary nurses an hour off here and there. Now his conversation has started to come back, but on Friday I could barely hear him. Once he said, 'sorry I'm so sleepy', eight or ten times before I could hear what he was saying. It's sad to see him struggling to repeat even the simplest phrases.

Friday 1ˢᵗ April (Good Friday)

After a walk with Louis to Keeper's Cottage, Caroline, Perceval and I had our usual banter over the toast until the phone calls began and we all retreated to various chores. Two Marlborough boys staying with us half turned over a Volkswagen on Hackthorn Hill: it had a burst tyre and a bent chassis and had to be towed away. P took an hour's Good Friday service in which I got to know Psalm 22. I had a wicked feeling my father would die histrionically at 5 o'clock, but in spite of an attack (which shocked the nurse as well as me) he carried on, rather unmoved by Parsifal and Passion music on TV. He politely sent his apologies for the service, but told the nurse continually that he would be 'coming down to the town' – sometimes the signal for her to help him into his chair or back to bed. Yesterday was sunny and he sat by the window for three hours watching the boys playing tennis or the cars coming down the drive: it's quite a commanding position.

A howling north wind has started to moan around the house, blowing away the Easter warm weather. It sounds most plaintive under the garden door and oak back door opposite the dining room. Garden visitors are arriving in thick coats and scarves and I feel I should congratulate them.

My father has been steadily improving. He enjoyed seeing Anne and Torquil on Saturday (fresh from a flying visit to Le Touquet for lunch the previous day). Gemma and Michael came for Sunday lunch. Simon Tuckey dropped in and my father was obviously pleased to see him. As Simon left my father again asked me disconcertingly if I would 'take over' from him (presumably in offering hospitality – he seems more conscious now of other people in the house) because he was, as he put it to us, 'going down now'. Under the bedclothes?

He and I had one or two friendly conversations during the weekend. In one I was looking out of the window. 'Quite a few garden visitors,' I said. 'Good.' Long pause. 'Where are they putting the money?' 'It's all right, Mr Clark's collecting it.' 'Oh.' And then a long pause. Finally: 'Who's Mr Clark?' I sometimes despair that poor Shirley and Stan will ever make it into his consciousness – a year after they have been here. He seems blissfully unaware of most other people until they actually come into view. At the same time he seems pretty comfortable in his room, tucked into bed by Liz, the current Maori nurse.

Perceval gave him sick communion today. Apparently he remembered most of the liturgy and listened patiently to all the readings without getting tired.

Monday 18th April

We got back from a week's skiing holiday this weekend and I came straight down here on Sunday, collecting the dog on the way from the kennel at Toller. Dorset has settled into a heavy grey mist, contrasting with the hot slopes of Savoie where even the glaciers begin to melt.

Water problems everywhere. We have had a ballcock rust through, with water pouring out of the main hot water cistern. The Puzeys have had a flood from overflowing bathwater – rather unlike them, I say to David teasingly down at the petrol pump. And then today I hear that Coltleigh and Holeacre farms have been out of water for nearly a week, while the Copps have struggled to replace old pipe in the field below the reservoir. The poor estate account has to bend again to meet nature's demands, none of which we can control; but at least the rents are in again, and my father has paid back his loan. His highly valued VM 1 number plate should be a valuable medical insurance, keeping him in nurses for a few more months yet.

He is making excellent progress. Julia thought she had seen a ghost on Sunday afternoon when he appeared in the library having come downstairs unaided, on some whim. As Mike Hudson says, he gets an idea in his head and follows through, regardless of any empirical experience. He is talking more like his pre-December self again: kindly and self-centred, replying out of good manners rather than genuine interest. My old resentments seem to rise with his convalescence: our conversations flash from warmth to chill, and we seem to glare at each other when we talk. I am astonished how he is picking up. He asks me if the car is all right, and I have to tell him, yet again, that it is being exchanged. 'Oh,' he says gloomily. When I remind him we are getting another car he brightens and says he may need to go 'down to the town' as if he is about to walk out the door. Perhaps he is. He is certainly mad enough. Mike and I almost chased him along the corridor to the bathroom. He walks smoothly along, though without any muscular power, as though he was simply willing himself into the next place.

This evening I battle with flannel weed, which has started early this year, even smothering a frog and a golden orfe in the top pond.

Monday 16th May

I've returned to Dorset after three weeks away, to a delicious warm early summer. Yesterday I drove my father to Hooke through multi-coloured hedgerows and bluebell woods. A fox crossed in front of us on its way to Ramsmoor and the rabbits seemed equally brave. 'Where are we going?' my father asked nervously as we climbed Warren Hill – which I took as the signal to return. It was the second of three outings this weekend, all part of his miracle recovery over the past few weeks, mainly in Kathy Picken's care.

We had two house tours, one local, one from Bournemouth. As I took them into the library, after stifling the TV, he got up and welcomed them warmly. I can't decide if it's nanny's good manners or a wish to show off the Burgomaster's chair that makes him stand up. The chair may be younger than the legend that Charles II sat in it, but it still has an important place in the tour so he is presumably adding his respects instead of remaining, as he sometimes does, integrally part of the exhibit. Either way the visitors are appreciative.

Janet, our temporary nurse from Bridport, says he was bolshy today. Reminded that he had felt a bit weak and had lost his appetite, he said firmly, 'Weak? I don't think so, dear,' with as much denial as politeness allowed. Last week he apparently said: 'I'm NOT going outside – I hate going in the garden', but with coaxing he'll say the opposite minutes later.

I managed to steer him out of the house through the garden door but after smelling the lovely rosa primula behind the wall he soon scuttled back inside and missed seeing the blossom in the churchyard.

The battle to save water lilies from the pervasive flannel weed rages on. No sooner are the flowers and fish freed and the weed cleared, you turn your back and the ponds are suddenly green again

Sunday 22nd May.

Convalescence is rampant and we wonder where it will end. My father walks happily into the rest of the house, pausing at the drinks tray and even helping himself, though we think we can counter that with apple juice. Old patterns are quickly re-established. He gets obsessed with missing keys and mercifully he has found his yellow drawer key. The 'new' Volvo is at last in the garage, replacing the Range Rover, and he has stopped demanding, 'Where's my car?' though he is now ready for expeditions ... and we dread them. I tried and failed again to show him the churchyard blooms. Yesterday, though, he came down to the Orangery for a picnic lunch, warm under the jasmine. We found a dusty *Private Eye* from his last regular visit last November. Today was his 82nd birthday. Julia and Timmy came for a coffee and present–giving and stayed for lunch, while we went over to see the gardens at Minterne.

Tuesday 31st May

Today a new nurse arrived to replace Sonya, the gentle Zimbabwean who has come close to being an adopted daughter. At lunch when she said goodbye my father said, 'Goodbye dear, all good things have to come to an end, I suppose,' and was obviously upset. So was I sorry, but I found she had a mysterious quality too. She was very interesting last night talking, for the first time, about the younger white farmers who were returning to recover their old land in Zimbabwe while their parents stayed away.

Also there for the night was a man who is writing a biography of Quintin Hailsham. He had one or two good conversations with my father, but most of the evidence came from his war diaries, which I have found in the muniment room – fresh with comment and full of quotations. This has given me a new interest in looking at my father's own papers which include confidential notes of meetings with ministers at various times, though I suspect nothing historic.

The writer went up to say goodbye and then, starting chatting in the bedroom about the Tory Reform Committee, very nearly missed his train.

This reminds me of a short discussion I had this week with Enoch Powell who was speaking at the annual Pepys Club service. He told me my father had had a 'Whiggy streak' in politics (at first I thought he said a weak streak) while he himself was a Tory. I told him I was working with charitable organisations in Africa and he said that was very Whiggy too, so I am a little confused. I suppose to him it basically means aristocratic and therefore paternalistic and idiosyncratic because founded on wealth rather than ambition or talent; in political terms it could mean almost anything.

Today we had a comic scene in the bank when he asked for £30 and pushed a ten–pound note across the counter as though it was a cheque. He started walking out into the road and it was impossible to hold him, but mercifully Caroline appeared and fielded him. I think he bought his fifth tin of lighter fuel in a few days (he doesn't remember even if it is on the library desk in front of him) and I wonder – again – what is in store for us, especially as regards other sorts of alcohol Earlier this week he insisted on visiting Pines, which is now an antique shop, presumably in search of the odd bottle of port, but he just stood there and stared unbelievingly at the window until Sonya coaxed him back into the Volvo.

We drove to Crewkerne and waited patiently on the platform in the sun for the train to arrive. He said it was just like the old days, and launched into the story of him and Drogo competing in the Huntingdon signal boxes. He said how smart BR carriages had become. Then he got tired of waiting and walked back to the car, negotiating a puddle, until Simone appeared – a smiling Brisbane girl with a backpack. Sonya went on the next train.

I managed to do two hours work this afternoon (on Southern African refugees) until I felt it was time to look out for my Indian guests – Minnie Boga and her Canadian husband Robert. Luke and I took Louis down the valley to test his retrieving powers, using the launcher, but promptly lost the baton in the bottom field. Minnie and Robert arrived, but as I was taking them upstairs Jeff appeared saying bullocks had got into the green gate by the goldfish pool. Together we managed to shoo them out quite easily.

I couldn't blame them for dropping in for a drink, only for droppings on their way out.

The rhododendrons and azaleas are looking lovely, especially the purple ones up under the trees on the bank. I wish I had time to do more gardening and even pond clearing, but my only contribution this week has been weed killer alongside the tennis court. Building works have resumed. The garden wall pointing is nearly done and the scaffolding should come down tomorrow. The Rectory stable conversion is coming closer with yesterday's visit from a digger, which has opened up an entrance and revived the field drains. Down at Burcombe the BBC has no less than 50 people involved in a few days filming of 'Rockcliffe's Folly', which will make a splendid contribution to rewiring that farmhouse. And a grassland society wants to have a barbecue AGM – on the gravel I hope.

Saturday 25th June

My father has continued to improve over the last month, and now even wanders along to the kitchen or the office to find out what's going on. We even 'allowed' him – however much he feels it is his house, we have rights too – to come into the dining room for dinner last night, but he picked at the smoked trout for ten minutes and eventually got up and left. I have started to censor conversations about him and his difficulties because they can take up valuable time and there are a thousand other things with an equal claim – he cannot be allowed to get away with the amount of attention he has. It is difficult when we have visitors for the weekend – this time my aunt Betts and her companion – because he demands respect that he does not always deserve. We are having wonderful warm weather and the boys have been clearing out the swimming pool and refilling it, at the expense of the precious reservoir and much shaking of Mr Kennedy's head. Yesterday an architectural historian, Ted Fawcett, brought a group of students and divined the water course through the upper garden, meandering in a curious zigzag towards the cistern known as 'Queen Elizabeth's bath'. He also 'walked through' foundations of an old byre behind the dovecote.

Monday 27th June

My father has succeeded in getting his cheque book back off me, after several attempts to collar the bank clerks, who smile away in obvious embarrassment. I have collected several of his cheque books, old and new, and piled them up in a drawer. So far he hasn't actually found any, but through familiar persistence he repeated his need so often I finally gave him one.

The problem for me is fairly basic – there is no money. This not a worry for him or the bank manager, both of whom will happily collude from their various vantage points. I know very well that any spare money is being eaten up by nursing bills, and he simply cannot expect to draw any more on an ailing estate account which can barely keep houses from leaking.

Meanwhile his constant thought is the bank: who is going to drive him there, and when, and how much he will take out. Last week he collected well over £100 but I scooped most of it up to pay Mr Kennedy. This may not work every time. Some notes are going missing – he has either handed them over to someone passing by or he has spent them without anyone noticing. The first seems more likely.

The dialogue is roughly like this:

- 'Johnny you couldn't take me down to the town, could you? I don't drive nowadays, I'm supposed to be too old.'

- 'What do you have to do?'

- 'Well I need to get to the bank and – a few other things – let me see (*fiddles with yellow labelled key, opens the drawer and forgets what he's looking for*) – I *need* to get to the bank, can you get me there?'

- 'You've got quite a lot of money in your wallet haven't you, from last time?'

- 'No, I don't think so' [*pained look while searching*], and so it goes on.

When actually drawing money he creates pandemonium, which even two of us can't sort out. Having finally picked up his cash he totters out into the road, smiling at faces he no longer recognises, if he did before. Beaminster people are kind to him, especially now that he's out of the lethal Range Rover.

Tuesday 5ᵗʰ July

I rattled into Crewkerne station at about 1.40 p.m. to find a reception party: a bent old man with a blonde nurse waiting for me, as I had semi-organised but not expected. Debbie, from Sydney, says this last week has been fairly uneventful and he is not stuffed with notes. Apparently the bank has even been brave enough to tell him there's nothing in his account. One reason he has eased off is that he has been drawing on the garden honesty box regularly, padding outside two or three times an afternoon to empty it and sometimes even beating Stan Clark to it. Once they arrived at the same time, inspected each other's keys and called it quits. I suspect Stan is leaving a bit in there so that he won't be disappointed.

He has forgotten the gardeners altogether, so there's little point in involving him even in paying Mr Kennedy as he always has. As for Jeff, he told me: 'there's a man with a brown beard in the garden' as though he was the spy from the game *L'Attaque*.

From the station we drove back over Toller Down, the route that I prefer on a fine day, but he complained of the length of the journey and told me it was much shorter through Beaminster. I let it pass. At Marsh Farm I was pleased to see builders retiling the barn and the hole in the farmhouse wall filled in. 'Who's the farmer living here now?' 'David Puzey', I said for the nth time. But then he doesn't really know his own grandchildren.

The showers held off and the Dorset Decorative and Fine Arts Society enjoyed their house tour and teas. One woman had last been as a wartime garden inspector, searching for new bean patches, presumably. Another man was an architect from Corfe Castle who had based a lecture on Mapperton windows – apparently a rare combination of styles – so I wished I'd mugged up on quoins and mullions. Two ladies arrived late, having gone to the wrong Mapperton (there are three).

My father refused to let us into the library and drowned my tour introduction ('four families here since Domesday') with some appalling TV jingle until I went in and turned it off. He has started a worrying new habit of wandering through the house while the tours are on and I feel tempted to draw him in as an exhibit, though it doesn't always work. Oh well: as a child I used to interrupt his house tours. I'm rather pleased with a new bad joke about pointing out the motto on the ceiling 'With swift but equal steps' – just as people negotiate the dining room step – it's about as bad as advertising cream teas from the church choir stalls. Eventually I do introduce a woman from Eype who has applied to be his companion-helper (a job we're having great difficulty in filling). He greeted her gallantly and said, 'Do come again, my dear'; quite unaware that she might very well do that. He said the same farewell to me an hour later, a pink rose in my button–hole, on my way to Yeovil Junction. A quick turn around the garden had allowed me to pretend that water levels would allow the golden orfe to survive one more week. On reflection, I am not so sure.

Friday 16th July

We had 120 members of the Dorset Grassland Society around the house last night, C and I interchanging as guides. I was hoping to cut tours to 15-20 minutes but C was still in the staircase hall when I was ready by the front door. The Clarks and I signalled to her through a doorway but she was in full flight – surprisingly telling the 'loyal' sandwich story, i.e. that the 4th Earl's other hand was free for naval paperwork and not gambling. One or two people went round twice to get two alternative versions of the tour; I know I improvise a bit, and discover I have invented John Morgan's murder in the dining room – it actually took place about 40 miles away outside Wells. I find I am lingering too long in the church, muttering about the stained glass which I know virtually nothing about. But they all seem to enjoy it and write to say so.

Afterwards the society had a lamb barbecue outside the stable by the ha-ha, professionally organised by Kingston Maurward College: 25p per head extra bought them rain cover (though it was a fine if windy evening) and a place for strawberries. My father made a couple of visits to the spit which obviously impressed him, and he didn't comment on the removed turfs. In fact he licked his chops and asked the organiser, 'if there's a little left over perhaps I could have it and make a contribution to the fete' – not being sure what the event really was, though there were some familiar local faces. The Alan Fooks' were there, obviously having a good time, and the Streatfeilds, to whom I suggested a possible Dorset Foods promotion here next year.

Saturday 17th July

I took my father over to Cerne to see his latest (18th) grandchild, Cosimo – 'not after the Medicis but because we like the name'. He amazed me by calling the dog by its name, Tushka. He had been confused all the way there via Rampisham and Wraxall, pointing vaguely home in a northerly direction. He recognised the ford at Sydling, but still grumbled about there being a better way. On the way back I gave in and drove him along the ridge past Minterne and Batcombe, with its lovely view towards Sherborne across the Blackmore Vale. We tried to recall what the baby looked like and I said I could never remember babies' colour of hair or eyes; and anyway Cosimo had a cold and wasn't at his best. 'Aren't babies' eyes always blue when they are born, and then change to brown or green?' he said.

Saturday 24th July

This weekend we have a very old friend of my father's staying – Gilbert Longden, formerly MP for Morpeth and later Hertfordshire, who was in ICI in India for eight years before the war. They greeted each other like old penguins crossing the Arctic to meet, and went happily into the library together, although Gilbert's faculties are much more intact and I was afraid he would get bored. Somehow he has managed to stimulate old memories we would never hear about, mainly of the House and old friends. Mapperton is shrouded in mist and rain and we have lit log fires and stayed inside like *Wind in the Willows* characters most of the time. At breakfast this morning my father was telling us about the General Strike but Gilbert was one up on him – and is actually three years older!

Sunday 21st August

We returned from a Channel Islands part-sailing holiday with the Tuckeys – mostly stuck in Alderney because of gales – arriving from Southampton station at about 7 p.m. via the back door. Margaret, the current helper, said they had been wondering where we were. 'When did you arrive, Johnny, I didn't see you come in?' – an old refrain. 'Oh yes, we've been here for some time,' I am now able to say. We have a sense of freedom walking in through the little back courtyard that feels more like our own territory. We are paying Mrs Clark's wages, we have decorated most of the rooms on this side, and we are (gradually) converting the kitchen. It may be puerile to assert this when in reality we have had the run of the house for five or more years, but it is a fact that we tend to stay on one side of the house and hardly use the Tudor wing unless we have visitors, in which case we now take over the drawing room which has been under-used. My actual reply to my father, though, was a cop–out. 'We had a certain amount of luggage to bring in so we came in the back door.' It is, as he well knows, just as possible to bring luggage in the front door.

Another reason was to see Louis, who immediately wagged up to us and jumped up, which is not normally allowed. The enormous pleasure of looking forward to seeing a one-year-old labrador after four days, rather than a dotty octogenarian, needs little analysis.

I am beginning to wonder if my affection for the old man is wearing thinner than ever as he recovers and will affect our general attitude to our work at Mapperton – which does not deserve the resulting neglect or harsh treatment I have tried to look back at his influence. Earlier today we were sitting at the airport station and the train was late. Caroline had a go at summarising the positive advice and education which he has passed on to me and which is now easy to forget. It is not a long list: European travel and culture, motoring (different from driving), some friends and Conservative contacts including two godfathers in high office, and model railways. I should add to this his interest in 'the Commonwealth' (though more of a nostalgic concept for him) and his 'good manners' which are undeniable though sometimes cancelled out by strategic bad behaviour. We were drawn into this subject because of the meticulous training and discipline which she had had, like it or not, from her own father – e.g. in sailing.

I sat with him for a quarter of an hour while he had his supper on a tray. I told him briefly about our abortive sailing trip, how we couldn't get out of Alderney harbour, about Queen Victoria's and Hitler's fortifications and our visits to tiny surfing beaches and rocky coves. Then I asked him if he had had a tranquil week with all of us away. He paused and thought about this and then let out a contented belch in reply. He said his 'housekeeper' – the name he always gives to temporary helpers like Margaret who never seem to fit exactly into the social order he has been brought up with – was leaving and he didn't know where the Volvo ('*my* Volvo') had disappeared. Then he fumbled for the key to the drawer where he keeps his diary and found the relevant pages. I find this a most arduous exercise, often repeated if any visitors crop up in conversation – and he said he didn't think anyone had been to stay but Richard Needham had come to tea. What was it Richard was doing now? 'He is still a junior minister in Northern Ireland.' Oh yes, he said. I had no family news to give him, with all our three children abroad. So with that the conversation petered out, and I went off to join Caroline on a lovely sunset walk down the garden with the secateurs.

Monday 29th August

This weekend the mists descended and the age of coal ended at Mapperton, with the oil-fired hot water boiler now installed and Mike Caplen no longer coming down to riddle it or relight it every day. We still have to dispose of our remaining coal but I have refused to go down and bag it, having taken enough exercise with the strimmer, in between the showers, during Jeff's absence on holiday.

My father is quickly adapting to Anne, his new helper who is a charming Zimbabwean girl. Today was her birthday and she has had a succession of African phone calls but very little time off, with our busy office life and Caroline's parents staying.

Anne is very tolerant and follows him to and from the honesty box, even three times a day on a sunny bank holiday afternoon –

like today. He probably forgets he has been out to it before, but after all a man's got to get income from wherever he can. I also suspect he thinks he is still competing with Mr Clark who used to cover for him when he was ill but has long given up the race. It also doubtless helped my father to shirk a tea invitation to the Talbots today, though he had other excuses, notably his back which has been giving trouble. 'You probably didn't notice, Johnny, but while you were playing tennis I was walking past with this charming girl, and just as I was leaving the tennis court I fell into a hole.' Yes, I did notice. Anne picked you up very expertly while I was staring through the tennis net, unable to move. And you groaned rather loudly in an exaggerated way which I'm afraid I often find irritating when you get in and out of your chair. And I could do absolutely nothing about it.

He is still a rather frail figure, but on the plus side he has become a rather more 'sociable' character again, occasionally trying to talk to people at lunch instead of always chewing noisily or monopolising the attention with idiotic remarks. For sanity, and for the sake of guests who may be staying, we still reserve supper for ourselves in the dining room while he has his meal on a tray in the library. We also have breakfast at a different time so that we are uninterrupted when he wanders past to see what is happening in the kitchen, though he does occasionally simply wander in.

We have reached some kind of house timetable and modus vivendi, but the future now seems more uncertain than ever. The level of time and energy required to keep the bills paid and the house and estate running, let alone satisfy an old man's modest whims and intrusions, leaves us gasping. We cannot afford the time and additional energy which he still demands of us, and we are unable as well as unwilling to share any decisions with him however much they may affect him. At least we have had our short holiday. We must now plunge back into the mire and prepare for winter.

Sunday 9th October

'And go easy on that vodka!' were my parting words. 'I will,' came the wavering reply from the hall as he padded back, with the first cocktail I've seen since November. Until this week his girl helpers have skilfully handed him apple juice after apple juice – brown enough to look like sherry and refreshing enough to stave off thirst. But now he is returning to his old form and seems to be fast approaching red signals. Yesterday I tried to stop him buying a bottle in the square. First I tried a heavy lecture, reminding him of his fall when he knocked over the electric fire, scorched the floor and nearly burned the house down – you have to lay it on a bit or he won't remember. But even then it doesn't sink in very deep. I tried telling Robyn, a fair-haired young nurse from Natal, not to let him buy anything except sherry in the last resort. Half an hour later they come back, with him clutching white paper parcels uncomfortably as he put down his hat. I get all ready to attack when I see the vodka and martinis emerge, but then realise there is no point. Let it be, as Caroline's father sometimes says. Actually you have no choice. Not five minutes later when he's forgotten whatever you say.

Caroline herself was very upset on Friday when I came down. There are occasions when each of us is bowled over by the impossibility of our situation down here, compounded by one old man's eccentricities and egocentricities. There is a terrible feeling of wasted life at Mapperton, however calm the surface and ordered the arrangements. The children feel it and resent my father for it though they don't understand how I, in particular, want it or have to put up with it. The emptiness of the house and the physical appearance of the kitchen, in particular, reinforce this feeling. Once redecorated it should become a warm centre again, but at the moment there is nowhere warm to sit except opposite him and the television in the library. Coupled with this he has started complaining about the cold – reasonably because the heating has given trouble – and goes endlessly to turn up the house thermostat, though his own rooms are quite warm.

The compensations are, for Caroline, the people who live all around us whom we see regularly and for whom we carry a responsibility. I hear his voice. 'Why don't you go and talk to George Brown sometimes?' 'Do you ever see the Fooks'?' Yes, man.

Friday 14th October

Jemima's 15th birthday, and isn't she marvellous? I came down on the train in time for the governors' meeting at St Francis School, Hooke. They've made me chairman of the managing trustees, which sounds important but basically means staying on for ten minutes after the full governors' meeting. The SSF brothers led by Bernard said it wasn't their style to be 'up front' so they would rather have a lay chairman. They fixed it quite cleverly and unconstitutionally in the tea break before I could even think about it, but it's only a formality – until I start raising difficult questions about the number of committees. I've also been hijacked on to the standing committee instead of buildings, luckily, because they've just started to discover dry and wet rot and old asbestos lagging under the staff–room floorboards. Ha ha, I mustn't laugh but we've been through all that at home and it'll cost a thing or two.

Higgy hasn't quite cottoned on to birthdays. It was Caroline's yesterday and I did a bit of prompting in the car on the way from Crewkerne station, but in the end Robyn and I got so fed up that she went and got cards and things from the chemist and we artificially created presents. Then lunch on three trays and the usual *dialogue des sourds*. Exasperation this afternoon because my father had asked Andrew Roberts, a young historian, to stay and has now suddenly cancelled him – a researcher who wants to talk to him about Lord Halifax.

'But I haven't anything to tell him, I don't remember Lord Halifax.' (Then why did you write him three letters and ask him to stay?) After ringing Roberts' answer phone twice I go into the office to find a message from him on ours asking us to cancel the taxi which must be already on its way. Stranger than all this is the way that none of us has spotted the 'three letters', either going out or coming in.

I spend a happy half hour reading out old news cuttings and taunting my father with his many strange utterances in the House of Commons.

Sunday 13th November

The first main shooting day yesterday – warm and gloriously clear. Christopher Pope comes over from Dorchester and I hear all about his expertly organised shoot where birds fly as though mounted on automatic metal antennae. How relieved I am that this is a relaxed, non-profit making part of the world where money is only an objective after it's too late to do anything about it. I realise how irresponsible a view this is, of course, but I think outright neglect has a lot to do with the quality of life. Perhaps I'm just suffering from good old suppressed envy late on a Sunday night when the children are going to bully me again into leaving half an hour ago. Oh yes, on reflection I obviously am.

The point of this diary was to record my father's various antics in the last years of his life, but now that his years are lengthening again it seems utterly useless to confine myself to him. My life has revolved enough around him already.

Yet here I am again, recalling him as though I still needed him strangely. And curiously, as I did the bonfire this evening, and collected sticks from the wood in the half dark, I was missing those occasions when we would be out in the garden with him and found myself wondering how he would have managed the same operations and whether, even, I was 'doing them right'.

His eyes streamed with tears as we watched the armistice ceremony on TV. 'Are you thinking of Drogo [his brother who was killed in the war]?' I said, and to explain himself he said, 'Yes, he needs a lot of thinking'. He was impressed by Prince Charles and said what a fine man and a 'fine character'.

I snatched some pictures of Keepers Cottage for use in the forthcoming court case, and wished the piles of scrap cars were even worse than they are, to make it easier for us to move the Ways

to no. 6. But it will be a long drawn out affair which we will win
in the end. I feel indignant that the Way family have exploited us
for so long, thanks to my father's conniving and feudal protection.

Saturday 19th November

I find that with both boys away I am actually, for once, the 'family
gun' – the free place in the minor day syndicate, and try to fit into
this role at 10 a.m. sharp outside the Old School. As I suspected it
is one of those easy-going minor days with desultory conversation
about the shooting form. But I achieve an early result even without
my glasses: my first shot of the day, close to the pheasant pen, and
not that easy through the trees. After that it was all downhill, except
for the walking which was the reverse. Then I go and leave my glasses
at the bottom of Holeacre. Timothy, my six-year-old nephew, comes
valiantly down the hill later in the day to help me look for them, but
we find nothing. On the way we hear Bobbie Brown whistling to the
pheasants at dusk and scattering grain for them, delighted at the ones
who have escaped. 'I don't like people shooting them,' she explains
to Timmy who is understandably mystified by the whole thing, but
likes the excitement. He finds a horseshoe beside Holeacre Farm, left
over from pre-war ploughing, and says charmingly that his eyes are
'peeling', i.e. well peeled.

The old man has been ringing the plumbers almost three times
a day and they are fed up. Cecil Tolman comes up as we are staring
into the space where the builders have hacked out the office wall for
a new flue – revealing an ancient arch in the process. We dislodge
a covering tile, allowing some rubble to fall into the old flue which
Cecil is in the process of repairing. He comes up and says 'that's put
the cap on it', so my father will have to lump it. I have left him a
fierce note. That very evening, we went out with Cecil and Dorothy
to the Crewkerne Concert band, an unforgettable evening of brass
and burgers, washed down with a lot of mixed–up EEC wine at a
good fund–raising price.

Sunday 27th November

'There used to be three pairs of nightingales around Copse Barn, but you never hear any now. Must be ten years since I heard the last one,' said Bill Guy, bewailing the onslaught of chemical fertilisers, and then going on to denounce the woodland school in Hooke Park.

Betts and I were sitting with Bill and Helen, in grandpa's old 'log cabin' which he left to them for their lifetime, looking out over Sort and Eggardon. Betts was more propped up than sitting. We had foolishly left her alone at home for half an hour at lunchtime. We had gone up to the school hall with the shooting lunch, while Jennifer Allan, our temporary Australian, had gone down to the Orangery with my father as usual for tea — now moved back to 1.50 pm, half an hour after coffee! One can only imagine how many times Betts had crept in from the sitting room fire to visit the sherry bottle, but it looks like about five good glasses. When we got back she was blinking like a frightened pussy cat lolling about in her chair quite unable to stand. I strutted around making all sorts of jolly remarks about fresh air and outings, having fixed up with the Guys to drop in for coffee. All the way over I breathed in what I could only describe as the air of a brewery cellar circulating in the front of the car. Eventually we reached Helen and Bill who seized her by the arms, knowing the situation (or similar ones) perfectly. She was finally sipping coffee and talking happily about her father's first building of Copse Barn after the war.

Michael Saunders Watson was over to shoot as Patrick Pisani's guest, rather full of the cares of historic houses and treasures. (He inherited Rockingham Castle from our mutual uncle, Michael Culme-Seymour.) It was a bitterly cold morning, and I took Louis out with the beaters. He behaved fairly well until I dropped the lead to tie up a couple of pheasants and then ignominiously chased after him the whole length of Home Wood shouting 'Ludovic'. I imagine most guns are used to Orlando doing this, week after week. I had to go in at 11, but I watched the bungalow drive from a chilly corner of the hedge near Holeacre. The pheasants literally scuttled past me down the hedge into the plantation – I thought they had escaped for the day but later heard that several were shot in the wood. The 'bag' was 75. Many more birds are shot at most other shoots every Saturday, so it's hardly a slaughter.

The von Neubronners, Michael C–S's cousins, were staying, heavy-hearted over struggles about their family graveyard near Stuttgart which his brother has bulldozed. Michael came to dinner to see them. He described his own problems looking after Mrs Barlow, his 'housekeeper', and the Johnston family's estate duties in Scotland. He seems to take on much more, even as he gets older, but doesn't seem any less able and active, I thought, as he drove off into the dark.

This evening Caro and I did our favourite walk round to the woodland garden, with some none too effective secateurs. Plenty of brushwood lying about, so as it was dry I lit a monster bonfire while Louis rampaged and put up several pheasants. As usual C insisted on seeing *the entire* garden, with the excuse that she had been in the Gulf and hadn't been here for five weeks. We walked back past the marching bamboos , the two duck, the small goldfish pool, and home, as always late on to the road back to London.

1989

Sunday 8ᵗʰ January

The Christmas holiday has nearly ended. It wasn't as bad as last year when my father was ill, but still seems like punishment. However there were the usual highlights: the brass fanfare at the carol service, and co-operative guests like Frances. Tristan, now at Bryanston, had a memorable if frustrating few seconds below Parsonage Copse, watching a pheasant passing a line of guns and finally pressing the trigger – with the safety catch still on.

Yesterday we had the annual family shoot – a rough shoot which, like the farmers' shoot, has been squeezed out of a crowded calendar. It produces no income – rather the reverse – and involves a lot of telephoning and walking. It includes one drive, usually with two or three beaters plus dogs. This year they were Nigel, Denis (Fairall), retired from Mapperton Farm and now working at Bridport –Gundry, and Kate, supplemented later by Jemima aged 15, plus assorted dogs. The guns included Nicky, Rob – who shot well with Nicky's second gun – and me, the younger gang being away or back at school. We spent the whole morning in Wytherston Marsh, nicknamed 'woodcock wood' because they always fly out of the rhododendrons at the top. By lunchtime the weather cleared and we had a brief sunny afternoon mainly standing under Home Wood waiting endlessly for our three beaters.

A glorious day doing next to nothing at all.

My father surprised me by enquiring after the game book which I have left in the muniment room – also the munitions room – in the vain hope that the boys would fill it in. I told him we had shot 14 pheasants and 5 woodcock – in fact a further 4 runners were picked up by Nigel and his dog this morning.

The bag is rarely a guide to a good day's shooting which to me is enjoying the countryside and the walking. However, he seemed satisfied with the result and I filled in the details back to December.

Sunday 29ᵗʰ January

Most of this month my father has suffered from back pain, and has stayed indoors. Some days he has even stayed in bed, but during the last week Shirley and the New Zealand helper have been coming in around 9.30. 'Ah, you've come to get me up,' he says, or else just vehemently, 'No I'm not getting up today!' I went to the library to say goodbye today and he was already upstairs, curtains drawn, by 4.15 p.m. I put my head round the door and he explained: 'I didn't have any more to do today, and there wasn't anything on television, so I decided to go to bed.' Fair enough. He said goodbye with a pinched smile and a thumbs up. He was in better form yesterday when Richard Needham came to tea and used his politician's bullying technique to provoke reaction.

The drawing room ceiling has finally been painted – a grey parchment colour – with the burst pipe insurance agreed by the loss adjuster nearly two years ago. Next is the staircase hall, but we can't face the disruption and aggro from my father at the sudden sight of Roy Copp's scaffold tower looming outside his bedroom like a mediaeval war machine.

Yesterday was the last shooting day, and there are great plans for 1989.

Monday 6th February

I took out the 'Beretta Special Mod' for the first time on Saturday. It is a present from Perceval (who has sold his Lancasters) to Orlando, who has carved a special niche for it in the red baize, no. 3 in order of precedence after the Hollands. Henry G–B's AYA remains in its case until Christopher picks it up this summer when he is 15.

Caroline drove Louis and me up the hill to the bungalow and we met George carrying a brace of pheasants by the feet – one way to pick up rat plague, he admits. We are going to build a new pen to replace the historic 'bungalow' which has always spelled thrills for standing guns. This is because we will soon be clearing the site for George and Bobby's new house, provided we can all think of a way of paying for it.

Louis and I then set off down the steep old lane to Burcombe, putting up unattainable pheasants. It was gloomy and damp but a glorious valley walk was guaranteed. The Fooks' sheep have improved the grass, but there is always felled timber lying about. The occasional pigeon broke, but well out of range, not surprising considering I was yelling at Louis every time he disappeared.

The gun felt light and comfortable, and I have got into the habit of running my fingers over the chequering which makes it safer to hold. Over the brow to Mythe there was a strongish cold wind so I went uphill to a favourite spot above the oak avenue sheltered by pines, and stood there. Louis started worrying about in a bramble, dirtying his nose in a badger sett. I looked across at Bentover Coppice where the combination of larch and pine made an unforgettable purple and blue – once painted by John Nash. No pigeons there, so on across the muddy plank over the stream and up into the wood, higher and higher until we reached the rides around the pheasant pen in 'Home Wood'. There are patches of fir or Lawson's cypress where I used to stand with my father and you can almost guarantee a pigeon, but every time we approached they were away. On across the water meadow and into the garden copse where I revived and then raked out the bonfire, and then home – without a shot being fired!

Easter Sunday, 26th March

Yesterday Mima and I took my father down to Beaminster to buy Easter eggs. I left her to steer him into the Tuck Shop and along the pavement while I went shopping, but I lost them. Apparently he had bought only a few mini-eggs and then wanted to visit Hurford's the electricians with his TV remote control, but for no real reason. Eventually they turned up in the square, just as the Hodgins and Pansy Wood appeared, so a cocktail party atmosphere developed. Mima then found a proper 'egg' for Caroline and we set off for home, passing Michael Fooks in his tartan beret on the way through Marsh Farm. A typical exchange followed, my father mishearing the name of his farm, North Poorton, several times. It's sad that even these very familiar names from over the hill are now almost meaningless to him.

But he came to Easter Communion, following the hymns and prayers quite closely. The church was beautifully decorated with spring flowers by Caroline and Mima. He was in the second pew with Caroline, with Mima, her friend Catherine and Deborah, the South African helper/ biochemist, in the front pew beside the lectern, and me behind them. John Hodgins and Jean-Alice gave the readings a North American flavour, and Perceval's prayers were markedly Commonwealth and Empire.

A lot of bramble slashing has taken place, with Perceval reminding me of the usefulness of burning, and me supplying the diesel. I have discovered a new 'grotto' under the hill, complete with lined channel, dam and waterfall, but everyone with an opinion (two Haymans in particular) says it is an old field drain – or rather a storm drain protecting the garden. Coming across the garden I saw a confrontation between dog, cat and duck, each apparently taking a firm position and glaring at the others.

Eventually the dog, of course, gave in. No more Jacob's lambs born, we are now 8 ewes and 8 lambs and look like staying that way as we usually do. Jo–jo, the black and white one Shirley has been feeding, now has his own little pen next to the garden cottage.

Over £100 in the honesty box today after a lovely warm, airless afternoon. My father managed to get out there for the first time this year, beating Stan to it and collecting about half of Mr Kennedy's wage packet. I am ridiculously proud of the new open-and closed notice, which actually seems to work although the same old quota of Shell Guide ramblers, looking for the posy tree which commemorates 1665 plague victims, continue to miss the right of way 'by mistake' and wander into the courtyard. I would if I were them.

I have tried to analyse my father's gaze when I walk into the library. He is always staring fixedly, however quietly you open the door, with an expression of mild alarm and curiosity plus lack of comprehension. His look gradually turns to a smile as he hears my rather forced greeting echoing round the room. Sometimes he turns off the TV; mostly I do; and quite often it sabotages my attempt at conversation.

Monday 10th April

I heard today that he managed to give the slip to the new South African girl, Michelle, on Saturday. He walked across the lawn towards the Orangery and slipped on the stone steps, cutting his hand badly. She got him to the doctor. Neither sounds very moved by it on the phone.

Sunday 23rd April

We presented him with the round silver lighter. We all had a go at lighting it and I only succeeded by pouring fuel on to the wick. Mima had Alice Wilkinson to stay – granddaughter of DCW or Denis, the Eton housemaster who once got me to recite half of 'Lycidas'. They had their picnic in a corner together (one of the fates of middle age is always to have to be with the grown-ups). Orlando and Louis made another group, he quite fairly but typically complaining about the standard Dorset 'shooting lunch' of hard bacon roll and bits of communal lettuce instead of the chicken and avocado wonders you get in civilised places. I then walked with my father down through the garden to see the baby goldfish, with glorious brief glimpses of the valley through camellias, acers and pine trunks. It's a stunning sight at this time of year, when the sun decides to come out. Back up the steep steps – we must get a wooden rail up, I keep saying – and through the hole in the wall to the back door. The new lines of lavender make this area much tidier and I have been strimming the long grass on this very steep corner, which reminds me of the moat garden at Rockingham.

During the afternoon Orlando and I went down to help the 'gang' to put up a new pheasant pen at Holeacre. George, Nigel, Robin and Philip were already there and we spent nearly two hours digging what earth we could out of tree roots and burying the wire netting to keep out foxes. The labradors skulked around us, convinced something was about to come out of a hole. There were a few friendly teases about Orlando actually turning out today, and he put up with them reasonably well.

A writer called Patrick Wright unexpectedly came to tea to ask my father about the Army's controversial destruction of Tyneham in the 1940s. I was surprised that he remembered anything, but he did, about the difficulty of reconciling local and establishment interests. He apparently made a progressive speech at the time, about patriotism requiring the land to remain green and pleasant. We hunted through the cuttings books but couldn't find much of interest. I was amazed that he was still pasting cuttings only three years ago and flattered that he had included one of my articles for the *Guardian* on Vietnam.

Friday 28ᵗʰ April

Arrived from the station around 8 p.m. to find a bonny, slightly agitated girl from Stellenbosch called Sandra. Higgy was in bed but had woken up very confused, thinking it was time for breakfast and had got Sandra to draw the curtains. The confusion spread.

His face was full of alarm and some determination. He threw back the bedclothes: 'I'm getting up,' but I stopped him to explain it was evening. 'That's what people say,' he said. 'The time's gone crazy.' I pointed outside to show it was getting dark and was almost willing it to get darker. He agreed. 'It's a dreadful morning. I don't know whether I want to get up, anyway the time's all wrong. What shall we do about the household? They won't know it's time for my breakfast.' I talked to him about the family and he finally agreed to stay put. I tucked him back in. Then a nice parting shot as I left: 'You can always come in here if you get confused.' Despite a wet Bank Holiday weekend and more back trouble he got 'the staff' to drive him to 'the Coast'.

Saturday 3rd June

Farce returned to Mapperton this weekend. It seems to thrive with my father's returning health. Caroline was out and I had taken on a 'shopping' expedition with Timmy (staying this weekend while Julia, his mother, is in hospital), Higgy and the dog. I was just pre-positioning them near the front door when the phone rang. It was Jean Hodgins asking for the 'Middleton log', the Hudson's Bay manuscript which she is trying to sell for us. There was new interest in Minnesota and she was trying to fax some information there. 'Do you really need it now?' I asked, dreading the answer. My father was already sitting in the hall with his coat on, and Timmy outside on his bike. I went to the library, put the log under my jersey, and just managed to intercept Jean by the back door and avoid my father's questions. This is absurd, but he is still capable of rousing the old fury and confusion in me in anticipation of some preventive action he might have taken years ago.

Down in Beaminster there was another illustration of this. Timmy (aged 7) properly reminded me that Higgy had to be accompanied to the shops. I double parked near the Tuck Shop, helped him out, but was then mortified to see him walk towards Crane's, the grocers.

'You can get your chocolate much more easily in the Tuck Shop,' I said but he grimaced and strode on. 'I want to go to *my* shop.' I had to detail Timmy to track him while I moved the car and waited while he queued. 'Selfishness goes on to the grave!' I muttered to Giles Wood bitterly through his passing car window. I lectured him again when he came out, all about two fat bars of chocolate. He gave Timmy some. The rest of us have to ask!

A piano teacher helping him as a carer last weekend stupidly tried to cut across Shirley's authority and almost scuppered our sailing holiday in the Channel. Luckily one call from me to Shirley from a hotel in Poole solved it. Methinks I complain a lot, but not as much as I could. My head aches. But I've had three very nice sets of tennis with Tom Oates who has also put in several hours cutting back shrubs and grass under the wall.

Poor Cecil Tolman was up here to service the boilers. He looked very grey and started mumbling. Caroline gave him a cuppa in the dining room. He is now in Dorchester Hospital. Shades of the housekeeper who is said to have bust a gut moving carpets at Hinchingbrooke during the war.

Sunday 4th June

This morning we heard snatches on the radio about the terrible massacre in Tiananmen square in Beijing. Our only casualty this week was the other Muscovy duck – probably to the same fox lurking below Home Wood. Timmy found a nest with a broken egg and later a dead mole on the edge of the lawn. We all looked at it, contemplating new waistcoats, and then my father said, 'Don't we want to throw it away into that bush?'– which we happily did. Pheasants abound: we passed a very elegant melanistic pair on the main road, out for their Sunday walk.

Sunday 18ᵗʰ June

Waterloo day and another water leak. At Caroline's behest Roy and I walked up the hill to trace the pipe up from the reservoir. I suggested going round one hedge but Roy pointed into a patch of nettles and we cut a straight line through them to a drain. We lifted a series of manhole covers until we found the leak just below Ramsmoor wood. Louis of course jumped into the muddy water and then left most of it over me in Roy's truck on our way home. We will have to get the digger in.

The other battle was with the ivy on the summer house and retaining wall.

I quite enjoyed this, gradually roasting through the afternoon and then plunging into the cold clear water and slimy sediment of 'Queen Elizabeth's bath'. Luke kindly brought the garden tractor and trailer down. He and two friends dressed up very smartly as Turkish acrobats for a party in Dorchester, commandeering various costumes from us and the laundry basket in the attic.

Cranborne Manor is apparently up for sale and some friends of ours staying, James and Jill Norton, have been over to see it, enthusiastic after reading David Cecil's own description.

My father declined to picnic with us in the Orangery yesterday, so we sat under the mulberry and later saw him moving slowly down the steps with Fran, his latest helper. He insists on wearing his old green tweed jacket and jersey underneath, even with the temperature in the 80s. Later on I was on duty in the office, went through to see him and found he was already outside. 'Just checking the honesty box, but there was nothing in it.' For some perverse reason I enjoyed telling him that it was Saturday and the garden was closed.

He has become quite a bit more independent this month, thanks to the sticky alliance of warm weather and Cadbury's: he now keeps four huge bars of fruit and nut locked in his drawer. He has asked for the car keys several times (they are now hidden) and demands to know why he shouldn't drive. He rang me up in London one morning to ask me to counter-sign a cheque book application. He even sent off a £30 cheque to Greenpeace, during the week when the Greens won a sensational vote in the European elections.

Sunday 25ᵗʰ June

The village took over the Orangery last night. That's an emotive sentence to describe a wine-and-cheese party, organised by the parish meeting in aid of the old school hall, in a classical Ham stone-faced summer house — until now a highly subsidised sanctuary for one old man for very short intervals of the day.

The party went fine. In the morning Alf and Dick and I carried the trestle table out of the hall. Dick was very protective of his table and didn't want me to fold the legs without his help.

Elaine had the catering perfectly under control and soon covered the trestle with a white cloth, cheeses and salads. The only hiccup was on my side: no electricity for the fridge which David had already brought down. Much scurrying between house and Orangery fuses, but it was quite beyond me and I called the Davies and Greenham emergency numbers: Steve was at a cricket match, and where better, on a hot midsummer evening. So we had to make do. The bottles stayed quite cool in the silent fridge, the guests rolled in and everyone was happy. Most of Mapperton was there, and quite a few from Melplash. Tim Lewis, in his stylish sun hat, brought his house party including the Bangkok Lufthansa manager and his decorative Thai wife and a daughter at Bristol Poly.

Earlier on Shirley and I chased the sheep into the next field, Shirley pursued and was even butted by the black lamb. 'It'll be mutton chops soon, Shirley,' teased Alf. We moved the trough and ran a hose to it, but the garden supply is still dry: the fountain spurted brown for five minutes and then died. The lower pool is half down, and we only have another week before we should take the fish out.

Caroline brought her mother down this afternoon. I have a strong memory of helping Sylvia down the front path, very wobbly but insisting on walking. My father looked frail coming out of the front door asking if he could help and I remember her looking him up and down and saying doubtfully, 'He wouldn't be able to help, would he?'

Sunday 2nd July

Sylvia spent most of the week by the drawing-room fire but my father pretended (or believed — how shall we know?) that she was always upstairs in her bedroom. When they met they could only talk for a few minutes before my father had to move on. He now has extended his appetite to butter biscuits and has a tendency to slip back to the small kitchen for extra supplies and even made off with the plate after Sunday lunch today.

Catherine Sowell is now down to help, to our relief, and has quickly got into the routine of feeding lambs, cat, goldfish and now bantams — elegantly parading round the churchyard. The pools are being cleaned out and the lower one repaired. I spent a happy hour yesterday wading through sludge and lifting out great swathes of flannel weed for Gary and Andy Copp to cart away in the trailer. Golden orfe and frogs tickled my toes. Jamie Koch came down from Holeacre with his fishing net but the water was too deep and black to catch anything. Bella, Mima, Catherine and I had a rare spell on the tennis court and I managed to cut more grass in the orchard. The hot weather continues.

Catherine then had a week on her own while Shirley and Stan were in the Isle of Wight. All was comparatively calm except the alarm went off inexplicably one night – my father sat on his bed and thought it was morning. She says he's also become so impatient during bank visits to Beaminster that he tries to open the car door on the move.

Sunday 23rd July

The temperature is way up into the eighties and Mapperton Gardens, as you enter the stone doorway smelling the sweet rosa primula, are brown, dusty and unappetising. Through the drawing room window I follow a garden visitor to the edge of the path and imagine (= hope) that he is suddenly refreshed by the sight of the green yew topiary and the two ponds beyond. One pond is now half full and the fish seem happy to be back and breeding. The other is barely covered with as much brown water as we felt the hydrant could afford, but I have had to roll up the hoses. I went up to check the reservoirs and found one nearly empty: a fluffy brown fox watched me and when I called, it trotted up to the wood at Ramsmoor.

The TV continues to boom behind the library window. My father is on splendid form. Anthony and Barbadee Meyer are staying and took him out to West Bay and back via Powerstock. He insists on wearing tweed jacket and jersey, and it's all we could do to get him to wear the Panama. He obviously enjoyed a visit from Timothy earlier in the week: 'What I like about young Timothy is that he has a logical mind. If he has a message to give me he comes straight up and climbs through my window.'

Sunday 13th August

Yesterday Mapperton's Open Day brought its usual blend of worthiness and melodrama. The Cancer Relief ladies took over the Children's Centre table while I was snatching a decent lunch, and a battle royal was only avoided by an extra table — though later on its legs were carried off, presumably by another rival group. Caroline stared through the drawing room window, halfway through a house tour, to see my father taking off across the lawn. She just got a message across in time for me to catch him by the steps, and resumed her tour during which she was told that the Nile suite of furniture was not by Gillow of Lancaster — one of our few certainties. Kate unexpectedly turned up for my house tour, and I tried to depersonalise it until someone asked, perhaps disappointedly, 'Doesn't anyone live here?' 'He does,' said Kate's gleeful voice. By 5 pm, the end of the last tour, Stan found my father wandering in the staircase hall asking pathetically,

'Is anyone looking after me?' He had put up with visitors in the house all afternoon and had been out to see the stalls, even buying a sub from the Dorset Trust for Nature Conservation. But he didn't, at first, recognise his own daughter.

This morning I joined him in the yard as he pointed out, painfully for both of us, how many things had got into the 'wrong' place, like chess pieces waiting to be returned to the start. What's 'my' car doing here? Whose is this? 'We' don't need that. He stood watching as I trundled ladders and machines back and forth. Then he had a quick peek in the honesty box. 'There was quite a crowd here yesterday,' he said confidently. 'Yes,' I said, 'they paid at the gate.'

C and I walked with the dog this evening through Mythe and Holeacre plantation. Two duck got up from the pond we had dammed, followed by Louis rather late. We also saw several deer on the stubble, a rabbit, and two squeaking buzzards, wheeling hungrily overhead.

Sunday 3rd September

Catherine has held the fort valiantly during our holiday in France/Italy and makes me feel we have complained too much — she seems to work effortlessly though she actually needs the two-day break she is now getting. She's been dismissed, ignored, shouted at, but somehow gets round him when she has to.

It's the anniversary of WW2 today so I start a conversation about the 1930s, saying how much I admired the bust of Baldwin in the muniment room. This bust is at head height under one of the bookcases. We brought it out of the drawing room into its proper historical patch, and it now makes a useful Edwardian centrepiece to distract the older-generation tourists — those that are not busy tripping over the step out of the dining–room or up the stone steps to the church.

Higgy couldn't remember, but thought he'd bought it through the family after the war. I read out adulatory passages from *Who was Who?* which he agreed with. He even approved the comment that

Baldwin knew nothing whatever about foreign policy. What if he had not handed over to Chamberlain before 1939? Could things have been worse? Later I thumbed through an album showing my father in Ottawa c. 1936: he was obviously the useful young man about Baldwin. I also found a letter from Lady Baldwin accepting an invitation from his mother to stay at Hinchingbrooke and saying: 'Hinch will of course make all the arrangements.'

Catherine has tried to get him to have baths twice a week, but he often gets out of it. The 'agreed' time is 7 a.m. – long after he wakes up. One day she found he was nearly dressed and said happily when she came in, 'It's two minutes past.' Another time he said he'd already had his bath and she retorted, 'Hinch, I won't have you lying to me.' 'Well, all right, I had a good wash.'

Monday 18th September

As we approach autumn my father has the idea that Christmas is coming and so he rings Tolman's, the plumbers, continuously to complain that the central heating is off. He now rings them at least ten times a week. Michael Tolman tells me they just say 'It's being dealt with' every time, but I don't know how or why they put up with it.

We have had our American cousin, Betty Kneen, to stay with her husband Tom who had his eightieth birthday yesterday. When I think of all the festivities which have gone into eightieths in our family, I feel quite refreshed: a few cards and a birthday cake, and the shortest of speeches from me. Meanwhile they have given us the brandy! They got on well with our old friend Harry Williams, who is there to give us moral support. All three wandered around the house and occasionally bumped into Higgy, whose refrain to me is always 'Who are these people in the house?' and 'When are they going?'; though they apparently had one or two brief chats too.

Friday 13th October

I came down yesterday during one of the busiest weeks ever. I had
Telethon and Buckingham Palace meetings, followed by an interview
with the Anti-Slavery Society, then Hooke Governors today and the
launch of Christian Aid's 'Hungry Farmers' book I edited in London
on Monday. In the midst of these are two birthdays – Caroline's I'm
afraid being neglected. Why is mid-October such a crunch time? Cold
weather, Friday 13th, night-time and the rattle of the last train out
of Crewkerne all seem portentous.

I can't make my father out. Years ago I couldn't get through to
him when he was unwilling or incapable of listening, and now that
he listens I can't get him to hear anything, let alone remember. Equal
sharing is long out of the window, if I could ever have managed it.

This morning I sat next to him after breakfast, then again while
he watched the Tory Conference, and now again through lunch.
Nothing. He sits there, eating heartily, with very little wrong with
him now; but he seems to have nothing in his mind, or nothing he
could express. I bowled gentle conversation at him, all too aware of
drifting words, the futility of logic, the risks of reviving perpetually
repeated memories, the dregs of old forgotten battles, the latest twists
in agonised trains of thought. The old family home — now, yes, a
school: 'Do they ever ask you to go and lecture there?' Yes; no; it
doesn't matter, I can't think about it, anyway you asked me the same
thing this morning/yesterday/daily for three years (please delete as
appropriate). Like the broken clock, the lost cheque book, the central
heating — all apparently simple old men's innocent anxieties, seeking
gentle easy reassurance yet inspiring in me a kind of dread of the
void, of the bottomless hollow.

He is, remarkably, better — clawing back time from nowhere.
He has started filling in mail order forms for Vodaphones, cameras
etc, posting them into our censored mailbox — Shirley's pocket.
Incredibly, he has lately been asking why there have been no replies.
And at lunch today he asked if I had got his letter, one which

Shirley had let through, to which I brutally replied just 'Have some more apple crumble'. It seems almost humorous to write about, and occasionally I see the fun of it when I can put myself at some distance. But most of it is grim. Here is the letter he wrote to us:

> '*I have been thinking about the disbursal of the Mapperton Estate Capital and Income (have you indeed?). With your joyful and increasing family you should have an increase in income, and I suggest that my income should be adjusted to provide for this. I presume that our tenanted farms should make this a possibility, and I propose a new arrangement for the income — namely 60% to you both, and 40% to myself.*'

Well, you should have thought of that in 1962, when I first took legal advice against you aged 19, or in 1972, after you put up proposals for splitting the family assets, or even in 1982, when years of wasteful wrangling with four or five sets of lawyers finally reached a climax. It was Luke, as the next generation, who 'won' that round. Today you wouldn't get 1%.

Sunday 22nd October

I show my father some photos I took of him recently, standing against the warm colours of the walled border across the lawn. 'Who's this, one of the gardeners? Who is it, Johnny, Mrs Clarke's husband? Who is it?' I waited as long as I could, curious what images he had, and then told him. He was aghast. 'No, dressed like that? Look at my face!' I remarked that he probably looked at it every day in the mirror, but he said no, he never looked at it. I stared at him and saw tufts of white hair around his neck and under his ears. I fetched my razor and hoovered some of the worst areas. Someone needs to do it early in the morning when he shaves — me when I can face it. No wonder, if he says he never looks at himself.

I have let one letter through – a subscription to the Dorset Magazine.

Friday 27th October

He came on the line this morning, agitated about his cheque book. 'It's me, it's Hinch, it's your Dad.' He sounded ready for an outburst so I stalled him with weather and family news until he told me calmly. 'They don't seem to send me my cheque book.' Just as well, as there's no money anyway, but he agreed he would write to the bank for one.

It arrived a few days later. Sue has been having problems because not only has he kept her out of the bank, but one of the bank clerks has started saying that he can take out what he likes. Luckily Catherine is back again this weekend.

Sunday 5th November

Jemima, Catherine, Caroline and I stood in the courtyard drizzle last night performing the Guy Fawkes ritual. Two rockets abandoned their milk bottle and swooped up over the stable block, screeched and fizzled. A few wretched Roman candles — no, only golden or silver rains C said — spluttered miserably on the mounting block. A few yards away my father, enviably, happily, snoozed.

This evening I disturbed him at 5 p.m. to replace his double glazing. I had taken it out earlier to get at a thousand flies. I swayed a little, perched on a stool as I lifted the panes back on to their hinges. I glanced back at him, but he was patient, watching out of the side of his head. 'Johnny, what if a storm comes, it's not going to blow the window in, is it?' Then a few minutes later, 'Are you shutting the window, I like to have some air coming in, you know...' Finally, understandably, 'Can't we do it tomorrow morning' — just as I had sweated to get the last one in place.

The storms have been pretty bad. A chestnut fell in the yard and limbs have been strewn all over the garden. Tiles have fallen off the north pigeon house which is now dangerous. Then last week part of the garden wall collapsed. The ducks sit on the chimneys, unmoved.

Sunday 19th November

I asked my father what he proposed to do for Robert's 40th birthday – rhetorically as so often now, thinking I would have to make the decision anyway. He gazed up to the ceiling rather desperately, smoothing his forelock, saying 'We'll have to do something rather grand, won't we?' I had worrying visions of noughts on a cheque, but he suddenly caught sight of the Reid bust of Rob when he was about ten, high up on the plinth between the bookcases. 'Do you think he would like that back?' Then he hesitated. 'Or would he prefer me to go on gazing up at it?' Without saying that I thought that extremely unlikely, I told him it was very generous but felt mighty relieved I wouldn't have to do anything.

The last week has brought back concern for my father's health and the old sort of 'Are we near the end?' anxieties which now leave me fairly cold. The end seems quite a way off. Refusing to take his pills has simply led to more back pain and endless moans which compete with the wind under the oak doors. He puts some of it on, but he obviously gets himself into awkward and painful positions. The doctor has muttered about hospital tests but finally persuaded him to take more pills again.

Catherine found him looking rather cast down at the Daily Telegraph souvenir issue this week and saying 'Churchill has just died.' Then a few days later outside his bathroom he said he had been to London (overnight?) and was feeling exhausted. On the other hand I still find him lucid when he has got 'into' a subject.

Sunday 26th November

Yesterday was Rob's birthday and he came over from Cerne to shoot. At 3.45 he came into the library and saw my father immediately point to a red ribbon I had draped over the bust like a scarf. 'Could you get a ladder from next door and take that down, I want to put my godmother up there,' he said, forgetting the whole point of the exercise. I got the boys and the Beveridges to come and watch, and

Rob climbed up to collect his present. He dusted off the cobwebs and asked 'Are you sure you want to give me this?' — suspecting my involvement. 'Yes,' I nodded vigorously and said it was all his idea and not mine. Luke helped Rob to put Queen Alexandra up and Higgy seemed satisfied. She looks a bit too classical for a Scandinavian girl who walked out with Colonel Oliver Montagu — which is how she came to be my father's godmother in 1906. But at least she is the right proportion.

Higgy decided to stay in the library all day in spite of a warm sun. We had a jocular lunch — overcooked chicken which Orlando loves to criticise while eating huge mouthfuls — and over coffee I told him about the Holy Communion service in Poorton: he was genuinely sorry to miss it. I asked him if he was feeling dispirited at all and he said 'What kind of spirits do you mean?' but later said yes he was, 'on and off'.

Friday 1st December

Last night Kate, Nicky and I were about to go to bed at 11.15. James and Sarah Best had been to dinner, telling us about winning a national apple juice competition. The house was pretty cold away from the drawing room fire. Then Nicky noticed that the TV was on in the library so we all four trooped in to find that Higgy had got dressed and was sitting waiting for breakfast. We gradually worked out that his bedroom clock had stopped at 8.30: he had woken, reset his watch and started his day, probably thinking it was late! As he often wakes up before dawn, the darkness fitted in very well. We stood around highly amused and made a joke of it for as long as my patience lasted. 'What are we going to do in this situation?' Higgy said when he realised, clearly enjoying the predicament. I started cajoling. 'I think I'll just stay here, it's nice and warm.' He snuggled back on to the sofa. We looked at each other appalled and I decided it would be best if we went to bed so that Catherine, the present carer, could have a go on her own.

I came down at 12.15 to find them still preparing for a long night. Then followed a bawling match: 'No, I won't go to bed, I'm quite all right here.' 'Come on, you're keeping all of us up and behaving like a child.' 'Why should I, I can bloody well do what I like in my own house.' We were also thinking he would fall asleep and fall off the sofa; and that the alarm ought to be turned on. Eventually we pulled him up to his room but he refused to take off his green corduroys and lay there sulkily, eyes closed feigning sleep as though waiting for a chance to go back down again. Catherine spent half the night listening to his radio through the baby alarm: it finally went off after 3.30. He stayed put for the rest of the night and got up, bright and breezy (Kate's phrase), at his 'normal' time of 7.30.

This morning we went in and he beamed as usual. 'Sleep well?' we said. He began to remember, and I felt it right to explain why he had been bullied and he said, 'Quite right. I went back to bed and had a good night's sleep.' Good for you: exploit your relations, constituents or whoever they are and tire *them* out as much as you can so you can sleep.

Saturday 9th December

A glorious sunny day, with an easterly chill wiping the smiles away. As requested by Nigel, I stood in the top field with Louis during the first drive, tapping my stick, absolutely frozen. I couldn't hear if pheasants were getting up anyway because of the sound of Les's power saw. Luke and Bruno were shooting, and apparently I made a decent enough bacon buttie for them at lunchtime – that's something. C and I had James Lang Brown over to discuss woodlands, and we did well despite his writing off a car on the way through the narrow road at Chilcombe. At the end of the afternoon Louis and I walked up to Holeacre to join the guns, who were muttering about low birds escaping into the plantation. The sun set behind home wood, and on the way home Louis put up and retrieved a perfect cock pheasant.

Higgy was still awake listening to some rubbish on the radio. Sadly Catherine is about to go back to Sydney for Christmas, but he still looks amazed that anyone else in the house either exists, or needs to help him. 'What's that, the visitors' book?' 'No, I'm filling in the game book – 76 pheasants.' 'Who was shooting? What's that book?' I read him out some of the guns, present and past, most in his own handwriting. Then I wrote him out a note: 'Please do not get up before 7 a.m.' This seems to be working.

Saturday 23rd December

On Thursday night I brought down Betts, my niece Caterina, and the dog – the first stage of the Christmas caravan. The kitchen has a delicious clean smell where the paving stones have been sanded and the Aga has been lit. The whole house still has a fine dust settling on every ledge and picture. Rooms had been changed at the last moment, so I took both ladies up to Luke's 'wing' – Luke being shifted upstairs again to his chagrin. Poor Betts has had to tolerate: a Tudor bed so high she has to jump into it; a cat mess in the loo which I cleared up; and a grimy bathroom with no soap. Cate seems happy enough in Robert's old room – a bit better than Verbena ward (St George's), I hope.

Yesterday Higgy was champing as usual to get 'down to the town', marching in and out to find a driver. I sat him and Betts in her car, one behind the other, not talking. Then I found that the fuse box had fallen out of its bracket and was dangling above the accelerator. When I tried to fix it, it started shorting. Higgy stared at it keenly. 'There seem to be some sparks,' he said gravely. I felt desperate but eventually lodged it on a shelf and it behaved, so we went on down to Beaminster. I wished I had had leading reins. Betts crossed the road to get light bulbs and when I turned round Higgy had disappeared into the chemist. Mrs Smalley tried to help him but his wallet was empty, so I bought soap for Betts and butter drops for him. He then set off at a pace across the square to the bank. We had just negotiated the traffic when I saw Betts crossing at another point so nipped back to steer her over. By then Higgy was already in the bank talking to the cashier who was dressed as Father Christmas and telling him he had no more money this week. The whole atmosphere in the Midland was festive: carols on loudspeakers, plates of Christmas cake slices and chocolates, cards and cheery faces. It saved me from a tricky confrontation with Ethel Way who appeared from nowhere. Soon both my charges were tucking into cake and toffees while I got Father Christmas to ring his Dorchester branch and took out the cash needed.

After that it was plain sailing: Higgy's Zimbabwean girl appeared from her shopping and took him home in the Volvo, while I drove Betts on to Melplash garage to fix the fuse box.

Wednesday 27th December

Some of the early mornings during Christmas have brought, as they should, surprises. This morning I came down at 7.45 to find my father naked from the waist down with Margot, his latest helper, trying to get him to put on his white silk long johns. 'I won't put them on, they haven't got any place here' (no hole). 'This is what I want,' fingering the correct tucks in a ghastly old pair of Y-fronts. Poor Margot was only trying to install essential 'damp proofing'. This was because, if I dare go on, Christmas Day had produced an unholy double before breakfast: Margot coming along the corridor saying he'd made 'a terrible mess in his bed' and Sylvia (Caroline's mother) minutes later calling us on the baby alarm to say she'd 'done biggies' – mercifully in the commode. What with the cat in various bathrooms we haven't done badly, oh dear – but it'll of course catch up with us all in the end.

I handed over Higgy's first 'present' this morning – the original watercolour for Mr Haybittle's postcards of the house. He seemed to like it and I propped it up on the bookshelf. Jemima has put all his Christmas cards up attractively in the shelves. 'When can we take all those cards down?' I reminded him how they got there, and that Jemima might mind. 'When is she not going to mind?' P stands for persistence, politicians and pig–headed.

Thursday 28th December

Today started at 5.30 a.m. with my father wandering along to the bathroom fully dressed and stinking of urine. The great hero of so many political sycophants. I staggered out: 'Don't you know it's only half past five?'

He followed me back to look at his bedroom clock. 'So it is. Oh well, I'm dressed now and I'm going downstairs.' Don't worry about the effect on everyone else in the house, you haven't got half a pea of a brain left to do so anyway, for 'onomatopoeia' read automatically peeing peer.

But this morning I don't find any of it funny. I went downstairs with him and found the house freezing cold, but luckily I had switched the heating back on last night. I went up and tried to sleep and considered the new theory that it is bedwetting which actually gets him up earlier every day. Even variable sheep subsidies over the radio couldn't get me back to nod land, so I eventually got up and had a bath, resigned to making his breakfast but not to having any of mine anywhere near him. I got to the library with the tray at about 7.45 a.m. and he beamed and then stared at it: 'Toast, yes, egg and bacon yes, coffee yes, marmalade, thank you Johnny.' A poofy smell accompanied the compliment, but he meant it.

Yesterday I felt clear-headed again. We were recovering from Boxing Day when droves of nephews and nieces and friends came for the family shoot. We were 30 for lunch and about 15 overnight until we packed most of them off in the morning – Caterina on the train, Luke with the Hunlokes to Wiltshire, and other Montagus back to Cerne Abbas. Later, after an awkward change of plan, I took Betts over to stay with Michael. Jemima gave us miniature stockings. The Golf, loaned to the boys, is unfixed and has also lost its exhaust pipe.

My father collapsed one day on the staircase after we insisted he had a bath; he also had some new pills from the doctor. With Jane and Shirley's help we managed to get him on to his *chaise longue* where he spent most of the day asleep, and the next day he was as fit as ever. An agency lady from Bournemouth came with her cat to look after him and turned on her heel and went home within minutes when she saw him and the house – we had a lucky escape. Sylvia has been up and down, very unpredictable, and in spite of a very helpful new girl called Stephanie we've hardly been out of the house. We have all been rather tetchy, but luckily Frances (Fedden) has come down.

Sunday 31st December

Today we have our Christmas carol service and the boys have decided to throw a New Year's Eve party in the Orangery. So far Higgy hasn't looked out of the window at the striped yellow tent and the groups of boys and girls going to and fro with hi-fi equipment, coloured lights, tables, drink and home–made sandwiches. We drew his curtains early and thought seriously about spraying 'frost' on his windows, but another part of me wants to confront him with it and get him into a New Year bad mood like me. The phone has been ringing constantly and London trains are being met. I have had a nice conversation while burning paper on the bonfire with some of Stan (Clark)'s grandchildren who asked me who the 'landlord' was (knowing very well). When I said me, they asked if that meant you could do what you liked. I speciously replied that it in fact meant you had to see if people were 'all right', meaning that you (the management) have little time to do what you personally want to do, and therefore it's the very opposite of doing what you like; but explaining this seems a bit killjoy, even in a diary. I have told Orlando his New Year bonfire on the far bank is going to leave a mighty black hole but he says fairly that it was already in one.

Meanwhile Perceval (Caroline's father) and I have been ringing around to find readers and already have one shepherd too many.

We have no brass band or singers this year – presumably occupied with other celebrations. However we have a harmonium-player. Caroline is so fed up, she says, she can only 'happily play Othello on the computer and otherwise curse the lot of them'. In the end both the service and the party went off well. By the morning when the drizzle set in, the few children who had abandoned or broken glasses in various parts of the garden, gate crashed or danced themselves into exhaustion had dragged themselves to bed, and 1990 could start afresh.

1990

Sunday 14th January 1990

Since then we have had a wonderful, restful weekend off in Lincolnshire. Meanwhile my father has continued to destabilise all those around him and has been getting up at strange hours and refusing to have a bath. With Stephanie – a sensible Bridport girl who is rehearsing with the local chorus of *Oklahoma* – doing her utmost to keep up with him, he has started going to bed earlier and then getting up for 'breakfast' at teatime. Shirley rang us very late on Stephanie's rehearsal night to say he wouldn't go to bed at all. C and I increasingly feel he must be left alone provided he doesn't create more mess. He is also walking more, and even went on his old walk round the wood past the Ways last week. He really is an impossible old man, and it's clear that I have very little affection left for him, which doesn't make it easier.

This morning there was another bath incident. Last night we set the alarm and put out the usual chair barrier with the 'Alarm on' notice. I also wrote out a special note by his bed saying 'Bath at 7 a.m. – please do not go downstairs'. At 5.30 Stephanie went down to turn off the alarm: he already had his radio full on so I went in and asked if he had seen my note. No reply, so I asked again. 'You want me to have a bath,' he said sulkily, so I said yes, at 7 a.m. –

and went ever hopefully back to bed. But by 6.15 we heard him coming out fully dressed. I followed him into the bathroom and started running the bath.

'I'm not having a bath.' 'Come on, it's not fair on the people around you, you simply have to have a bath.' Caro had meanwhile appeared in a dressing gown. 'Hinch, you smell, you've got to have a bath.' Vehemently: 'I am not having a bath, I'm going downstairs.' Me: 'You're behaving like a 5–year–old.' He grabbed his stick and started moving towards the door, but we blocked it, and eventually he shrugged and gave in and started undressing, so we left Stephanie to it and went back to bed.

I could hardly sleep, though. The amount of time this man takes up, either directly or indirectly, is out of all proportion and we are now thinking more seriously of taking him to a nursing home. It's not that he is unmanageable (yet), but that he constantly takes time away from other important things we need to attend to. Nothing was mentioned at lunch but he was a bit sullen, complained of the cold and stalked off without apple crumble, leaving us happily discussing Hong Kong immigrants and a Caribbean journey the boys are planning. The boys were very relieved to see him go and I am worried about the effect of his depravity – there is no other word for it – on their attitude to him and the elderly in general. They resent him. Naturally C and I feel we should be able to share all our moans about him with them, and it's bound to rub off.

The afternoon disappeared too quickly. Caroline, George, Nigel and the boys walked over possible areas for future game cover, while I went to tackle more of the real and metaphoric brambles on the tennis court.

Sunday 28th January

Last Thursday's gale has left a trail of broken tiles and slates across the lawns and outside most of the farmhouses. The drive is strewn with twigs and branches. Roofing sheets have blown off barns, and the thatched barn at North Poorton has shifted several feet. I spent most of Saturday picking up slates and fallen branches.

'When are 'the men' coming to do it?' my father asked plaintively. Seeing us outside, he had come out of the garden door in the staircase hall. We stared up at the holes in the roof, knowing the rain was coming in. Copps had tried to stretch canvas sheeting over them but the wind had blown it into the air like a spinnaker. 'They have got a lot of old ladies to help before they can come and help you,' C said. 'We'll just have to wait for our turn.'

Electricity and telephones came on and off during the weekend. The generator refused to work. The wind continued to howl. The guns got soaked on the last shooting day, though the shoot dinner went ahead very successfully last night. Orlando has been doing some expert canvassing of his ideas for expanding the shoot and combining it with Combe Down.

Saturday 3rd February

The gales have continued and more branches have fallen. Kirsty, our new gardener, has made an enthusiastic start, clearing up the drive, designing the 'wedge' border beyond the lawn and getting lessons from Jeff on the garden tractor. The Rectory Stable should soon be ready for her and Chris. Meanwhile hard core has been laid down opposite at no 5, waiting for the dreaded Way scrap yard to move there.

This week's problem has been the rain. Gallons have been pouring through and around drains and pipes and under the south stable, through David's workshop and the sawmill. An inch or two of snow this morning left a white landscape but soon turned to slush and caused more flooding. Shirley was to be seen walking valiantly into the blizzard with a bucket to feed the Jacob's. I went on to the roof to try to locate the leak above the children's room, without success. More water has been getting into my father's bedroom, Orlando's room, the library and elsewhere. Towels, removal of pelmets, climbing ladders all give one the nice feeling of having 'done something'; but we are still waiting for Copps to repair the roof. My father is in high spirits and hasn't complained once today. Stephanie has even got him to have a weekly bath.

We had another long discussion about the shoot with the boys, who are aching from injections, being about to take off for the Caribbean. C and I went for a tour of the raging torrents around the garden – George has dug various trenches to free the reservoirs – and allowed Louis to chase his last pheasant. The others then had to drive on to London, narrowly avoiding floods outside Yeovil, while I went up to the parish meeting. The agenda seemed gentle until suddenly someone mentioned water, and everyone seemed to have it – on the road, through someone's cesspit, carrying away gravel, everywhere. At these times I have to hold on to my seat!

Sunday 4th February

I crawled through the roof this morning, but the wind has luckily dried most of the water out. I climbed up to replace various light bulbs and met my father wandering pathetically, saying 'I was just looking for a little nourishment, but I can't find any sign of my apple juice. What's that on the roof, flapping like a tent – I should have thought it would catch all the rain.' He still has an uncanny, useful knack of spotting danger, because sure enough a cord holding the tarpaulin has snapped.

Monday 12th February

Another storm throughout the night, but this morning it is calmer and sunny. Water has been lying in pools in the garden and branches are lying everywhere. During the weekend C and I did a tour of damage and unblocked several drains. Timmy and I went up to the attic roof and found some of the slate and slates wet inside. He and I spent nearly two hours in freezing rain, clearing the gravel path under the beeches. This morning I went into the garden just in time to see seven fallow deer, one white, nibbling the border under the pines below the round pond, clapped my hands like a governess and watched them escape over the fence up on to the lynchets and stare dolefully back at me. Mercifully there are no more trees down, though one has apparently blocked the Poole–Dorchester road since Caroline passed through last night.

A wonderful letter with several catalogues has arrived from the Wordsworth Trust, asking if they can borrow Cozens' 'Grande Chartreuse' painting, the romantic Alpine monastic scene visited by selected English 19-year-olds after the French Revolution. I was fascinated to learn for the first time that Wordsworth adopted Basil Montagu's little boy for a time and brought him up near here at Racedown Lodge c. 1795. I took the correspondence in to my father in its original parcel form on the Father Christmas principle – why do I bother unless it's somehow me, the parent, enjoying watching the bemused child? 'I don't know where to put it, I don't want to read it and I don't need any of it.' Betts was staying and later on when she came downstairs I gave them both a short lecture under the painting.

He has been in generally good form considering 'Le General Février' has been one of the most tumultuous wintry opponents he has ever had. With the roof scaffolding up we have thwarted several 'When are the men coming...?' questions, and he has displayed a surprising level of acceptance of his situation, admittedly without very much understanding.

We watched the momentous news from South Africa surrounding Mandela's release and I tested him on his attitude at the time of Sharpeville and the first treason trials. He said he had thought then (the classic Tory view) that the blacks were too simple and unready for government in the 1960s, but he now (like Margaret Thatcher and the rest) apparently accepted that change was necessary. How cheap such attitudes are worth for their owners, and how many other people's lives have they cost?

C and I went over to Marsh Farm cottages to discuss the state of the roof with Guy Gale, the thatcher. It's so bad that he says he averts his eyes, and the gales haven't helped. Water is seeping down into the timber and stonework, and we have to do it. The sight of it has given me added zeal in ringing the head of Sotheby's this morning to ask why it has taken months for them even to estimate the CGT on the sale of family papers. I have a vision of the water eventually trickling down the wall into the muniment room, soaking the last valuable manuscripts and with them the livelihoods (plural) of Mapperton. At the same time it's wonderful to think that a thin sheet of parchment can now fetch a thick wall of Ham stone.

Saturday 17th February

Dione Digby and her daughter Zara came over this morning to discuss a Music Society concert we are planning to hold in the church in July 1991. They went in to see my father and Dione sat beside him and talked flowingly about mutual friends and her various projects. He recognised her then, but by lunchtime had no idea who had been to see him. 'Who was that lady who came here and sat on the sofa and held my hands and gave me kisses?'

C and I walked round the house with Raymond, looking at possible colours for down pipes – we decided a creamy yellow which would blend with the Ham stone. Raymond said he wished he had had a camera yesterday when Copps were replacing the old battens on the north roof and laying down felt and slates – he said it had looked like the wreck of a great ship. We went up to see the Old Rectory stable which now has a smart fireplace and polystyrene cornices. To everyone's amusement, C has kept the original open drains in the flagging. The main bedroom and bathroom upstairs are very attractive, too. We spent the rest of the morning talking through the various jobs which will need following up after C goes to Saudi Arabia next week.

Sunday 25th February

So much to be done, in the office, on the telephone, in the garden, but I am refusing to be diverted from what I enjoy doing too! This diary for example is an unjustifiable use of time but it helps me to sort things out and recognise the important or interesting bits.

Meanwhile the wind continues to blow and the roofs shudder. This week's calamity was the pigeoncote which suddenly lost a 3-foot honeycombed west wall, now covered in blue canvas and flapping eerily. The huge pile of stones and mud show how thick it was, perhaps because so little lime was used. One assumes it was built to last exactly 324 years which it has.

The north roof is now almost complete with tiles. Roy Copp was on it on Friday when Ethel came along the drive and grumbled about her new cottage. 'I won't be there long, I can tell you.' She repeated it to me the following morning and I felt rather reassured.

I went down to Hincknowle for drinks before lunch with Joan Best, and chatted about Romania to Alice Dilke and saw the usual crowd from Evershot to Chideock – not unfortunately including our MP Jim Spicer whom I had wanted to rope into the South Africa lobby on Tuesday. The Observer has Nelson Mandela describing how prisoners were buried up to their necks in mud on Robben Island and then peed on by prison warders, yet says he has never hated white men. I wish, though, that he and the ANC would get on to devise new policies and ideas before the world loses interest.

For once no one asked after my father, which was refreshing. He himself continues to be in very cheerful form, which is just as well. Mima and Catherine (just back from Australia) collected Tilly from school and both girls got helpless giggles during over-formal lunch conversation. Tilly is about to do ancient civilisation among other A levels, and wants to go to Nottingham or Manchester university via Italy, India and everywhere else.

Trees continue to lie about, fall over or drop limbs. The spring garden is strewn with branches among the daffodils and I ought to be out there now, with Kirsty starting as manager next week. With George's help I have compiled a list of lost amenity trees for the DCC. He and I have just lifted a huge fallow deer he shot into the back of the Passat and he told me — as he does every time we meet now — about more trees down in this or that copse or across this lane or right of way. He will have a look at two which Maureen Legg told me this morning are preventing their tractor from crossing the stream below Burcombe.

We have still heard nothing from the Bromovskys about taking Holeacre but I will chase them. A major keeps ringing up the answerphone from Warminster about barn owls — I wish C was here to talk to him.

Saturday 3rd March

More branches strewn around the garden but at last the wind has dropped. Several lambs have appeared and sadly two have died — Michael Fooks says we need a lean-to now we are lambing in colder weather. Shirley and Catherine are going out regularly to feed and check them. 'The lady fox,' Shirley says, is roaming.

The honesty box went out for our first open day; we are concerned about the effect on my father's banking arrangements. I took him down to Beaminster this morning and found him very distrait — he wandered up and down the pavement, stopping at the chemist and Crane's without going in. 'No money,' he explained, and I got him back to the car when he saw the bank was closed.

George says there are five beech down at Mythe and some Douglas fir along at Hankmoor. The tree above the stream is across the track and will need a digger. We talked about a new letter from the Rivers Authority and he said his cattle will be clear of the farm in a month — sadly the end of Coltleigh as a working farm. He suggests we go easy on the shooting arrangements with Combe Down but Robin is only back next weekend.

A strange conversation with Vanessa Clark who tells me that Don Giovanni, during the performance she's asked us to tonight, will be seen fully unclothed in a playground and will Jemima mind? I doubt it. I must go outside for at least 15 minutes to get the bonfire going. The Bromovskys are back and do seem to be interested in Holeacre.

Sunday 25th March

Mapperton people are footnotes, not makers of history – according to the last issue of the Dorset County magazine, which goes on to quote 'Victor Montagu's campaign against the Common Market'. Caroline feels it may soon need correcting...

Steps and the tap of a stick are heard coming down the passage towards the kitchen. A shaky voice announces: 'I only wanted to say that I shall be having lunch in the dining–room today.' Turns and exit right. He is much as ever during lunch, confusing every sentence of conversation. This afternoon he was watching 'Bridge over the River Kwai' and I was trying to remind him of the story but it was hopeless – he could hardly even remember Alec Guinness, once such a hero. He has no idea of where the rest of his family are and I was thinking of drawing a chart: it's not easy. Luke and Orlando are in Barbados, Jemima in Leningrad, Jesse in the US, Sarah in Italy, etc.

We joked at lunch when we were looking at the tapestry and he claimed the oak chest underneath had been in Huntingdon and we explained it was Caroline's. The right length for a person to lie in. 'I'm going to put my shroud in it soon, Higgy.' 'Oh no, darling, I hope not.'

A red letter day today: Kirsty Fergusson has finally arrived to be our first full-time garden manager, living in the Old Rectory Stable. I ceremonially swept her garden path and handed her the broom this afternoon. The house looks sweet, but it would be better if she had some electricity. [Famous last words. No electricity came and she has returned to London furious.]

Friday 30th March

I am in a state of mild anxiety about nothing in particular, at least something unidentifiable, and not for the first time in this house. I sit and try to think but for a few minutes seem quite incapable of doing or remembering anything. It feels like queasiness and aches in my head and stomach. Now then, start again.

My father and I had a pleasant lunch together and we talked in the library afterwards. He was quite vividly remembering Hooke and outings in the pony trap to the village and picnics in the woods. He suddenly asked about Brampton and the family vault, saying again that he would like to be buried there. I found myself phrasing the words carefully, too carefully, asking if he would like me to write to the church and find out if there was room in the vault. He said he remembered the steps down but then, charmingly: 'Would it have to be so deep, I could go just beneath the surface.' I said, Did he think I should investigate?, and he said very slowly in mumbled words: 'I should think I might be justified, after being called to judgment, in going up to heaven.' I roared with laughter, which was perhaps inappropriate. I'm still not sure, but I think he was making a serious case, maybe on my behalf, for not being buried at all!

The yellow chicks are delightfully fluffy, but need to take the air, and Stan is knocking up a run for them. The oil tanker crawled round them and the ruined pigeon house to fill up the tanks this morning. I have been stuck in the office and need to get out too.

Monday 9th April

He came into the kitchen this morning while I was gulping coffee, rather late at 8.30. I heard and dreaded the deliberate tone of his steps, knowing what he was after. 'Could you take me down to the town, I haven't got my car and I need to get to the bank.' No, I couldn't and you don't. I saw two wrinkled eyelids barely hiding two tightly focussed blue-green laser beams of steely determination. Then I said:

'No, I can't this morning, I'm too busy, you'll have to go down tomorrow instead.' I was poised for further enquiries about what I was doing that was more important than him. But in fact he nodded gravely and retreated.

A broken clutch cable has put his car out of action. But that poses no problem. It's the bank that irritates us. Last Sunday he slipped through the net and opened the honesty box, filling his pockets with a warm afternoon's takings. Yet he insists on fattening his wallet from an overdrawn account. We are all incensed at the raid on essential garden money but are incapable of preventive action.

Stealth seems to be the best course: removing the 'garden' notes from his wallet overnight at the risk of his remembering them. Confrontation simply exhausts all concerned and rarely stays in his memory. Reason is a non-starter, though we still try it. Catherine was in a crusading spirit today, hanging out washing in the sun, until she thought through the consequences. These tiny campaigns have to be followed through almost beyond the horizon.

An Arctic wind has blown away the sun's warmth. Still in some pain, like auntie in the 'ruthless rhyme', from my fall from an apple tree on Monday, I have been sweeping away dust and grit from the front path. Caro has been in a 'new broom' mood as well, fighting for space between her mother and the estate detail, losing some, winning more this time. The negotiations over next year's shoot are relentless, with one party sorrowful, one party bumptious. Jemima, on the phone from Leningrad, is bringing us back a samovar for Easter.

Saturday 28th April

Folie de grandeur comes only too easily. Looking through the office window I see a reflection of the Orangery on the bank just behind the pine trees and think how nice it would look there, perhaps as a guest-house.

I am in terrible disgrace. The Volvo 'ELF' is missing from the garage and Higgy has been told more than once that Catherine is meeting her brother at the station in it. But, woe, stay awhile, he cometh down the staircase full of wrath. 'I want to know what you've done with my car, you've taken it without my knowing...' etc, etc. I stared back: 'Are you angry?' I said. 'Well, yes I would like an explanation.' I paused and must have sounded smug. 'I'm afraid your memory doesn't serve you very well.' I explained this further as we walked into the library, knowing full well that Jemima and Lucy had gone off with the others to the sea. He was covered in embarrassment and apologized, and sat down to watch another instalment of Peter Brook's *Mahabharata*. I went in later and the TV had changed to the funeral music and superbly photographed ships in Odessa harbour in *Battleship Potemkin*.

Friday 3rd May

I have been thinking about nakedness. Nudity, *nacktheit* – does that ring better? In the heat I took Louis down to the pool this evening at around 8 p.m., leaving Catherine and Kirsty playing tennis. I was wondering whether to swim with nothing on – but it was still bright and the Daltons could easily have seen me from the Garden Cottage. I remembered my father's lack of inhibition in the past (that could easily have put me off), and many enjoyable 'skinny dips' in the canals near Hinchingbrooke, in rivers in France, off Bembridge at night, in Dorset coves – and much later with the children near Aosta, but that was different – and very cold. Childhood is so much purer in the memory, one can almost taste the water – and the experience remains fresh. Doesn't everyone wish they were like an amoeba sometimes, without hang–ups, floating blissfully free like one of the sea anemones in Edmund Gosse's *Father and Son*?

Saturday 4th May

It was a lovely surprise to see Caro early this morning, arriving at breakfast flushed as though she'd been for a long summer walk. In fact she'd driven two hours from Sussex after getting up four times

in the night for her mother. This is a weekend of old gentlemen –
Gilbert Longden and Nigel Fisher with Patsy, Bill Crawford and
his wife coming in to meet them, and our old man trying hard to
stay in the clover and avoid all of us. I kept him up until 5.30 p.m.
waiting for them. I got him to retrieve some new memories of the
swimming pool house at Hinchingbrooke which sounded like an
Edwardian summer house under the trees below the rose garden. It
must have had a flat roof with a skylight because he said the gardeners
continually climbed up it to remove leaves and branches. When I
started to play there in the late 1940s there was only an outline of
turf on the lawn, like a new grave.

My father grew more and more impatient, eventually asking,
'Must I stay here, I want to go to bed,' so he went up (did I let him
go up? – no, I couldn't have stopped him) but the guests arrived
just in time to wave up to the window. Watching his friends smiling
at him this weekend, amused and sympathetic, I have had a strong
feeling of the twilight of his life. Later we all watched a long trail of
bright white cloud behind an aircraft, like a comet coming out of the
sunset, passing us and disappearing. Then another came from the
south and crossed its path. The wisteria is at its best, and the scent
of that and wallflowers fills the house day and night.

This afternoon brought a lovely surprise. Mowing around the
tennis court I suddenly spotted another bright red vehicle coasting
in from the drive – another Mountfield come to help? I stopped
under a flowering crab apple and there was Joe Larcombe, happy at
the controls of a 'Battricar', 200 yards from home without his sticks.
I had never seen anyone so liberated in old age – a strong contrast
with our ageing lot. 'saw 'un in a magazine,' he explained cheerfully.
'Goin' down there in a minute' – he pointed down the valley past the
house to Keepers Cottage.

Caro said Sunday was one of the best days she could remember.
Those are worth having. It was a warm Bank Holiday weekend. The
NGS Open Day brought a full car park and over 200 visitors. Chris
and Kirsty organised a table and a money-box, and we did a mini-

census of visitors. VM tried to collect but we were all watching him. He and a few old men – a batch of retired MPs and an admiral – sat in the heat over their coffee. C and I walked round the upper path, pointing out the dead trees and shrubs we still have to clear.

Saturday 12th May

My father plods harmlessly through the house but I avoid him now except for brief library visits, usually suggestions for outings with 'his' (our) guests whom he doesn't remember are staying with him. Shall I pick up your coat and stick, or will you get them – you've got little else to do. Must I say hello and goodbye? He seems happy enough, even now that Catherine has left and only Shirley is there to look after him. He still gets bacon and egg – what more do you want of life? The feeling that everything around you is yours? Perhaps there is a real property-owning issue between us – the irony is that he has never believed in a joint family trust and continues to condescend to the rest of us. Do we care?

The Kennets stayed and we had a sunny if distrait picnic with my father in the Orangery, trying to get him to remember if he had once pinched Wayland's electric trains.

Saturday 19th May

I wouldn't take the housekeeper's job here for anything. I am on duty today and the most exasperating thing is him coming in to check on what you are doing. You hardly get the bacon and egg in front of him when you are told he needs to go 'down to the town'. All this on top of early rises at 1 a.m. (anticipation), 5 a.m. (alarm switch) and 7 a.m. (breakfast). It really is outrageous what one man can demand.

I am far from the ideal carer. I am actually quite unsuitable because I do not even want to sit next to him. 'Are you having breakfast too?' Well I can just about bear to take my cup of coffee in to talk to you for a few minutes. Very few. 'What sort of week did you have?' 'Oh nothing fantastic or terrible.' Good for you – or everyone who runs after you. Lucky no one comes in the window to knock you on the head. I sometimes feel like it.

I snatched a few minutes in the office only to hear him hammering on Mrs Clark's door, 'Is that you dear?' 'It's Mrs Clark's weekend off, I told you to wait until 9.15 as usual.' 'Well who's going to take me?' I decided to tease him mercilessly. 'Well now, what are you going to do about it, you'll have to work it out, you've been in much worse political situations.' 'Then I shall drive myself down' (stalks stuffily off while I call '9.15' after him). Impossible.

Friday 1st June

Several times a week, for some reason, I think of what Higgy's reaction would be to things I am doing if he were more 'with it'. For example, I'd like to tell him the story of my being 'summoned' by Princess Anne to the VIP room at IBM to thank me during the launch of *Prospects for Africa's Children* on May 2. He'd enjoy the glitter and I would exaggerate: this modest brand of snobbery is something we – I can hardly phrase it – both share. There are so many subjects that we have had in common but no opportunity to discuss as equals. This has been true, except for a very few occasions, since I started to go my own way in the mid-60s. Mercifully, I feel certain Luke and I are not going to have this problem.

I had a letter from him in London this morning which has escaped the net – perhaps secretly posted in the VR letter-box (C and I used to call it 'Victor Rex') at the top of the drive: could I go to Bond Street and pick up more paper for the barograph. He was given this as a 21st birthday present by old Lord Montagu of Beaulieu and we've moved it nearer to him in the hall window. Actually the spare papers are right underneath it. But the letter was very well composed, delightful to read; and to ignore.

Monday 4th June

He has now got into the habit of coming down for breakfast at 7 p.m. instead of a.m., having gone to bed at 4 and sometimes earlier, only to wake up thinking it's early morning. He has done this once before. Today Caro brought him in a delicious supper, a tray of fish, salad and toast with a glass of wine, but he said: 'I don't want that, I want my normal breakfast.' Not a chance of your getting that, me old mate. Yesterday, as a preventive action, I tried to get him to have his old snooze on the sofa after lunch, and he agreed. Janet and Richard Cooper and their three little girls were here and we lingered over our steamed apple pud after he went out. Minutes later he was on his way out with hat and stick. 'You promised you'd have a snooze.'

'I know that, but I'm not going to, I don't want to, and I'm going down to the Orangery.'

What if he wasn't at Mapperton? What would the place be like without him – just the same? Aren't we in control of our own destiny? I try and work out the pluses and minuses sometimes because the day will eventually dawn. Is he a useful security guard, or more like a potty old *chowkidar* shutting shutters in mid-afternoon, possibly saving a few pictures from sunlight but creating a kind of Hades for us. He glares at the garden visitors rather as he did at a bird beating relentlessly on his window today before going out to lance it with his stick. If he was a friend not a father and I ran into him for a chat in a corner of the garden, we might get on rather well.

I showed him a picture of Uncle Hinch and Edward VII in July 1906 from the Hunts local history magazine. We agreed the reason for the old man's satisfied look was less likely that he had had a new heir that summer (Victor) than that the King was sitting in his garden. In the same issue – which I didn't show him – is a gripping account of the last months of the 4th Earl's life in 1792 when his creditors, terrified of probate, were fast closing in on him.

Sunday 24th June

This man is exasperating, he is driving me slowly mad, he is of course himself insane but only about three of us know it and it's not possible to certify him, but by golly I feel like it. This is me speaking to myself in a controlled sort of way, the therapy of the computer on a very cold foggy Dorset day.

What has happened – as I've just complained to Kate at length on the telephone – is that he is starting to get up every day in the evenings, once or even twice, waiting for his 7.30 a.m. breakfast which we refuse to give him. This evening I went in to give him a sleeping pill, but he wouldn't have it. 'What's that, no, I don't have them.' 'It's because you are waking up in the evenings, to help you have a proper night's sleep.' 'Wake up, when, what do you mean? I don't wake up until the morning.' It's not worth going through my pathetic, repeated attempts to remind him of endless recent short conversations in the hope that something will click. It won't. I foolishly mention 'the household'. 'I'm not disturbing anyone, am I? No one's complained, at least not to me.'

Let's forget about him for one moment. What else is happening?

Maureen Legg came in to say that she and Gordon are going to make a go of the farm after all, sell the cattle and concentrate on ewes and hope it will satisfy a new bank manager. Caro, Giles Wood and Michael Fooks had a good tramp over the proposed game cover. The Jacobs lambs are growing up fast although the orchard grass is running out. We received the other Jacob's lambs, the Rothschilds, for tea yesterday after a lovely lunch party at Chilcombe. There are plenty of things going on which have nothing to do with a 'crazy mixed-up kid', as Jeremy Thorpe (whom we helped into a taxi in London the other day), once described my father with surprising accuracy).

Sunday 8th July

Today is the World Cup Final and the last day of Wimbledon – the first really hot summer day. Louis and I went up to the woods to get away from the madhouse and see the new pheasant pen, nearly complete. A few fallow paused in a clearing to look at us. Louis stared back uncertainly. We walked behind Keepers Cottage – the garden still wild because of the change of tenants but I can see colour near the back door – and Louis leapt into a trough to get cool. 'Where pants the hart...' Back past the repaired pigeon house, smart with its four new window holes. Stan tells me the heron is back, pursuing the new goldfish Mima and I bought in Battersea Park Road. Mary Soames came for a drink with the Peytons – very nice and in full flow. Higgy assured me he'd be there to see her at 6.30 p.m. but was in bed as usual at 4 which was bad luck for her.

Sunday 15ᵗʰ July

One of the most confusing 24 hours ever spent here – but for whom? Us, one old man, or everyone else? We have a film crew and Giles Brandreth, 'Discovering Gardens' for TSW. We have all the children, and Andrew and Jackie Best. Sylvia, very frail, with a New Zealand nurse called Marie. Louis. And all the Fooks hay-making opposite – the only sane ones. And the Daltons' alarm going off.... I'm sure we can cope.

At about 11 a.m. Higgy decided it was bedtime. Mima brought the news as we were catching up with each other in the office – the place where we get our breath before the next onslaught. This sounds emotive but the day began with a battle after Higgy appeared at 7.15 – the first time he has actually walked into our bedroom – in search, of course, of bacon. Caro hit the roof quite rightly because Shirley has been getting these visits too. They are not unnatural in the context of his desire for self–preservation, but they sure knock us sideways. I tried to remain calm and he explained that he was only looking for 'evidence that breakfast was coming'. He is a master at false modesty. Reason isn't even a word that can be used here today. He came in later looking for his hot water bottle, collided first with the film crew looking for a kettle, then Andrew and Jackie seeking toast, and then the boys getting up....

Sunday 29th July

I went in to him this morning with another kind of breakfast: boiled egg (a bit hard), compote de fruits and toast. He was watching 'Mister Men'. 'I thought I was going to be left to starve,' he said, giving me a sickly smile. 'Why should you think that?' I replied tensely. He lapped it up, and started to ask if I had any spare time, perhaps to talk, but I managed to get out before answering.

Yesterday I was greeted with a similar comment: 'I can't think what's happened to the staff today.' 'Staff?' I say frostily. 'We only have Mrs Clark, who is the housekeeper, and she's on holiday. I'm doing your breakfast.' 'Oh. Thank you very much.' Same to you. You may have dementia but don't let's confuse that with your endemic egotism. Equally the fact that I may have some of the same characteristics should not blind me from telling the truth about you. I yes of course realise that this one-sided conversation is entirely for my own benefit – it wouldn't get under your hide, anyway. Oh dear, why are we so roused by him?

Poor Gordon Legg nearly went up in smoke last Thursday when a spark from his tractor set his hay bales and half the hedge alight on the lane by the Loscombe turning. The fire brigade brought this dramatic news to Caro in the middle of a house tour and said it took 400 gallons of water from the reservoir to put it out. After two scorching weeks we have now got a refreshing Scotch mist. The pool is a delicious milky green and we, Michael, Jemima, Timmy and Sophie, the au pair, have all swum in the last day.

A day or two later John Dalton at the Garden Cottage suddenly died of a heart attack. Valerie called to him from the garden while he was reading his brother's legal review and he had simply fallen over. Jemima, Caro and I came running and tried hard to resuscitate him but we were too late. We were all shocked and sad. Our caravan holiday together had to be cancelled.

Sunday 19th August

Just back from our Greek holiday in Pelion – one of the best. I tried a boiled egg on my father again this morning and it seemed acceptable. He is in excellent form, which puts our strain level up, almost to the point we left it in July. Apparently he has started abusing Simon and Stan because we have started Spanish terracotta pot sales and have moved the honesty box and notices to the 'shop' in the corn shed, which has confused him. But they say he only mutters about it and they don't seem bothered.

On the way back from Beaminster yesterday I asked him about his father and he replied: 'It's a very long time since he died and I can't remember anything about him now.'

Sunday 26th August

Perceval took a 4 p.m. thanksgiving service for John on Thursday. Most of 'us' were there and a bevy of Benedictines came over from Downside where he used to teach – including a roguish Father Philip who of course P had known in some previous wickedness in Wiltshire. Over the sparkling wine and cake he and 'Gervaise' told classic stories of running into pupils in the Soho demi-monde: Hello Sir, what are *you* doing here? Val Dalton and Caro did some marvellous, vast sprays of flowers.

My father's new timetable continues, to his consternation. At 3.20 it's shutters and curtains – we now trip behind, muttering, and reopen them because it's impossible to influence him without energy-wasting. Yesterday I tried to stop him going up, hoping for a glimpse of the Test match (India are clocking up six centuries) – and he paused for a moment and said very reasonably: 'But I don't know where else to go or what to do...' A couple of hours later he is dressed and down again, ready for breakfast, and doesn't really want ham and salad.

Because of the boredom factor we decided to take him down to Melplash for the service today. Halfway through we had the 'Peace' and started shaking hands with each other and he picked up his stick and hat to go, thinking it was the end. But he was persuaded by Caro to stay and go up for communion (P was helping a retired bishop with it) and seemed quite happy thereafter, firmly reading old lines over the new Series 2, and why not?

Wednesday 29th August

Today was le jour de France at Mapperton when we received two groups of 33 *'randonnants'* from Paris, Lyon and elsewhere, led by my old Saharan *mehariste* and guide from 1966, Jean Soudriez. I told them over-enthusiastically outside the front door that 'we were all French here already' because of the Conquest. Little reaction from the first group; the second laughed, feebly. This was the sort of hit-and-miss result I had the whole afternoon, trying to create a French version of our tour, with valiant last-minute help from Chris Booth (*meubles*) and Kirsty (*jardin*). C wondered – after all this team effort – if they might really prefer to hear about English things. But they seemed to 'ooh' and 'ah' at Hortense Mancini's bare bosom (in an oil painting).

My French sentences being longer, each tour took 3/4 hour, though I had said 1/2. I had just let the first lot out of the church door when I had to rush round to find the second, standing restlessly outside, and Stan rather relieved. It was 4.15. I led them in to find my father closing the shutters on us, so I hustled him upstairs and started on Bonnie Prince Charlie's campaign. The seascape in Samuel Scott's painting suddenly darkened and egad, there was *mon père* on the landing drawing the curtains. I dashed up to draw them back and went hastily on to the story of *le sandwich*, French simperings in my ears. Unwisely I expanded on 'Madame Labouchère's' (highly accented) glorious 1920s 'renaissance' ceilings. It got so late by the time we reached the church that the sun had left the stained glass and down came a cloudburst just as they were leaving the porch. I rushed back again for umbrellas and helped them into their coach and up to the village hall. Five minutes of Shirley's cream teas, and all seemed well until water suddenly started dripping from the roof. I caught Jean's twinkling eye. He has always enjoyed the sometimes desperate plight of the *milord*.

Friday 7th September

The eve of the courtyard fair. Louis bolted across the field to become a silhouette in the evening sun, spotting two dogs on the footpath, and it was hard to get him back. I discussed the roping off with Cliff, the Sea Cadet chief, burly and efficient — basically to keep the cars away from the gundog demonstration. Back in the garden, shouts come from Mima, Catherine and Shirley under the mulberry tree.

Most of the day has revolved around the stable cleaning, the siting of the Dorset Harvest tent, the unobtainable megaphone and the unattainable skittle alley — eventually borrowed, at a price, from Broadoak village hall.

Saturday 22nd September

It all worked out, thanks to the team of Matthew, Nigel and George who laid on painted wagons, trailers for skittle alleys, clumps of greenery for dogs and every sort of moral support. Caro, Kirsty and I carried out chairs and plants. Mima and Catherine managed the 'loss leader' — John Hodgins' word for the bouncy castle. Chris and John and Derek pulled in the real money. Bobbie and Kate Adkin made the stable ring with teacups and loose change, and by the end we had £426 to hand out to Beaminster churches and other charities.

Then last week we had 35 for fork lunch from the Samuel Pepys Club. Louisa luckily catered for them, and with Richard Ollard's advice I laid out the 1st Earl's journals on a chest, showing the chocolate recipes and his elegant drawing of Compostella.

This weekend was all quiet by comparison. I came down early for a Telethon meeting in Bridport, and tried to fight off a lingering flu. I had a very enjoyable three hours with Peter Allsebrook and others from the Telethon in the Youth Centre, handing out about £26,000 of other people's money. It sure is easier than your own.

I joined Hinch and Betty for a model 'children's' lunch where we discussed naughtiness at Hinchingbrooke c. 1920 – a safe subject, one which they love and which holds their attention...just. The main story was of pinching nectarines from the kitchen garden behind Prouting's back – Betts of course being the one who got away with it. Then the horses – Hinch gave his up because he could never stop it bolting. How hard it is to keep these two souls amused, though they compliment and provoke each other innocently, almost charmingly. My father always ruins these occasions by deliberately changing the subject and asking me some annoying question such as, 'Do you ever go to Hinchingbrooke and lecture on the family?'

This afternoon I took them on an outing to Seaborough Manor, influenced by landscape architect Harold Peto. We reached the Old Rectory garden (found in the handbook) but typically Higgy refused to get out. 'I don't want to go on careering around the countryside.' All right, it's true we went via Melplash garage and turned up a few lanes: Betts liked it and so did you. Happily the owner, Willy Wright, immediately told us he already knew how difficult Hinch was, having been on the end of his, among other MPs', letters at the War Office, c. 1945. 'Hinch was one of the worst.' Betts and I ambled round his garden, under a fine four–storey Georgian building and then we all drove back.

Earlier I had asked Higgy about his excellent picture of Churchill lighting a pipe. 'I forget whether he gave it to me or sent it. I think he must have been throwing things out.' This is translation because he actually said something like 'ejecting his leavings'. Sadly I sometimes forget the quaint and often idiotic phrases my father uses.

Sunday 23rd September

I came out with Louis this morning to breathe in the very clear air. Valerie Dalton came out to meet me and a miracle occurred: simultaneously, all the ducks gathered in a circle around the dog, while a few yards away about twenty black-and-white pigeons flew down and surrounded the bantam cockerel. We marvelled, and dog and cock walked off rather embarrassed.

Friday 28th September

This morning my father got wind that I was taking the car to the Telethon meeting in Plymouth and was bristling. I confirmed that I was indeed taking it. 'What? My car?' Two years ago I would have reminded him that it was on the estate account and he'd have corrected himself: Well, all of us's car. 'Well, how am I going to get around?' Then I burst out, making no apology: 'You'll just have to stay here today because I am going to an important meeting with TSW Television.' There have been so many 'important meetings' of his in the past, and I still catch my breath before announcing one of mine.

Sunday 30th September

I heard a rattling in the staircase hall and expected to find him shutting up for the night. In fact he had locked himself in the library and was trying to shake the lock. I called out instructions through the keyhole and eventually he got it open. Minutes later he started locking us out of the front door as we said goodbye to the (Michael)Yorkes. You have to be perpetually on guard, as with a teenager or a puppy.

Looking down the garden from the lower pool you almost have to forgive him everything. Here is glorious autumn colour bursting down the valley, reds, greens and yellows, and it's all because one retired and sulky ex-MP planted up an orchard which he is now too old to see.

I had two enjoyable experiences with the Yorke children: yesterday, giving (7-year-old) Marcus lessons on 'driving' a garden tractor and chopping dead shrubs for the bonfire without cutting his ankles, and today, taking Jessica (at first with her mother) on a 'Tudor' tour, showing her the roof, ceilings and secret doorway, offering over-arduous explanations, then turning round to find she was no longer there!

Sunday 7th October

We took the Hailshams on board David Mowlem's frigate at Portland and lunched with him and Kay in the Captain's cabin. The tall policeman at the gate was very amused to see us coming the wrong way out and to point this out to me reprovingly, '…and with a senior member of the Judiciary on board, sir'. A delightful weekend during which I took the two old gentlemen slowly round the garden. Harvest festival and supper, only marred by Dick Powell's having stitches in his head after an accident this morning – a minibus ran into him.

Thursday 11th October

Arriving late from the station Shirley and I saw 17 pairs of eyes gliding across the car park – a huge herd of fallow presumably looking for autumn berries. They seem to be getting braver, and a lot of shrubs are being damaged during rutting.

Friday 12th October

I woke with the alarm going off at 5 and couldn't sleep on. A brilliant October day and I was determined to walk to the Hooke Governors' meeting at 2.15. Within 24 hours I have to be on a New Delhi flight, so time is vanishing. I drove my father down for the shopping run and tried to get him to buy birthday cards for the girls – with only partial success. No 21 has some delicious china cherries in the window but no one is allowed to buy them. Distracted by these I hadn't noticed him already halfway across the main road to the bank, just before opening time. I hared after him and managed to steer him back before the door opened. Then I picked up groceries, chatted to Angie Dupont, and we returned uphill, passing the blind corner where Dick crashed a few days ago. He is still black and blue.

So far so good. Andree did a competent sweep after me and through the filing tray and the morning disappeared into routine letters and bills. During an interval I showed Nicholas Rodger the c.1720 oval views of Hinchingbrooke with lords, ladies and grooms relaxing, and talking to a scholar I felt transported in time. We had supper together last night and I caught up with his research. Apart from writing the 4th Earl's biography Nicholas has given very helpful advice about appropriate manuscript sales, since we hope to turn most of the 4th Earl's official papers into farmhouse conversions, of which I am sure he'd have approved.

I left the office in perfect time (I thought) for a planned walk to Hooke, but suddenly the plan fell to pieces. There was no one in the house. The phone rang, I couldn't find Shirley or Stan and my father had also vanished, scattering unsigned cards. I leapt down to the Orangery like Basil Fawlty and faced him through the window. 'Other door,' he pointed. 'I've come to say goodbye,' I said (I'd already been through this once last Sunday, so why do it again?) 'Where are you going?' 'India.' Not an easy word to turn away on. The minutes were going; the walk was becoming a run. He stared, and I felt sorry for him. 'I haven't been to India for 30 years.' 66 years, I knew, since he had been filmed playing chess with Sir Edwin Lutyens on the voyage home after the completion of New Delhi. And then he said, deadly serious: 'Are you staying with the Viceroy?' I gave in and decided to take the car. Ten minutes later, there he was again, plodding down the drive towards me. I waved without stopping and saw him in the mirror looking grimly after me and thinking, 'Isn't that my car?'

Saturday 10th November

I tried to stave off flu this weekend – the bane of UK–returning travellers – by joining in an excellent fish meal last night at the Riverside in West Bay. Luke was in splendid form, talking away about friends and New York and shooting. This morning I still felt mouldy when I got up to do my father's breakfast. I ignored the fresh mushrooms and did him the standard boiled egg with a miniature marmalade from Heathrow – the nearest thing to a present from India. I declined an invitation to join him, saying I was going to the office. Recently he has been asking us more frequently to drop in and keep him company. Going in for a chat is one thing, but we can't bear to watch him eating with a toothy grin and a drip on his nose. As a result, no doubt, he's becoming just one more lonely old statistic.

I admit I often try to avoid him, snatching cereal and toast standing up, hoping to be finished before him. This morning I confess I heard him coming back with his tray and fled upstairs like a child, fearful of being seen. He pottered along below me and listened and called 'Mrs Clark' rather feebly, with no chance of being heard. Perhaps he had heard me. He started towards her door but as it is her day off I stopped him in time and agreed what I already knew, that he wanted me to take him down to the town.

On his way up to bed he stopped and pointed up at the McEvoy painting of three children [sadly one of those since lost in the 1997 warehouse fire]: 'that's you up there, with my brother Drogo.' Here was a rare example of transference – perhaps I have finally succeeded him *in vita*. 'Where are you then?' I should have asked, but said instead, 'No, that's you, not me.' Luke was behind me and said, 'He's gone, hasn't he,' seeing the remark even more eschatologically than I did. I had to agree: 'Yes, but don't tell anyone else because he makes a very good night–watchman.'

Saturday 17th November

This afternoon I was 'summoned' as I was chatting to the Powells – he had told Caroline: 'I'll make John take me to Bridport.' This was an oblique reference to my having agreed to take him out after the shooting lunch.

In revenge I drove him the other way, up towards the Wash Hill drive where I knew the guns had gone. He moaned as we passed the bungalow and groaned as we parked in the yard at Coltleigh. 'Can't we go back, I don't want to get mixed up with the guns.'

We watched two guns and heard a couple of shots, and then I relented. On the way out we saw Bob Gilbert with a water diviner in luminous overalls, so I explained to a puzzled Bobby Brown that this was to find her new water supply. My father failed to recognise either of them. I think this social failure is really behind his worry about meeting the shoot. After all these years he has turned his back on his old loves.

We went via Beaminster and I picked up an Independent and was delighted to find Richard Needham on the front cover, holding up Mrs Thatcher's umbrella in penance for having called her a cow on a carphone; this can only help his interests under a new prime minister. My father insisted on finding the house of Mr Potter, the dentist in Bridport, but when we arrived he wandered sadly along the pavement, trying to remember why we had come. After he gave up I took him into the little Unitarian churchyard next door and we had a nice chat to Janet Harrington, a nurse who is usually either sailing in the West Indies or riding a horse near St Tropez.

On the way over Jack's Hill my father suddenly said this was his favourite place. I had never heard him say this before. I looked along the misty coastline and the dual outline of Pilsdon and Lewesdon, with the sheep grazing in the foreground and the bright evening light on the clouds behind, and had to agree that he had a point.

Sunday 9th December

In the last two days we have had heavy snowfalls and intervals of bitterly cold wind and bright blue sky during which the whole Cooper family, plus Jemima and her friend Lucy Jay, and I have been on sledges. I even put on my Attenhofer skis and appeared unexpectedly in the middle of the Coombe Down shoot. I waved at Giles and one gun asked rather dryly if I had put wax on. Luckily Louis' sorties were into the wood behind, and he picked a pheasant off the track and we got away behind the line. Guns blazed and the birds flew on, expertly driven.

Peter Claydon and Steve Scott came in for tea and lectured the old man on getting up in the night, telling him he must try not to go to bed before 6 p.m. I reminded him it was his doctor speaking. All right, he said, he would. I asked him at once what time he wanted to go up this evening, and he replied with his old charm: 'Well, after that wonderful tea, and seeing you, I think I'll go up now, let's see, it's now 4 pm.' We all fell apart, laughing and defeated. But with their encouragement we are pressing on with the idea of having a gate at the top of the stairs.

I tried to get him to do Christmas cards, using the 1981 list which I have whittled down to 16. He insisted on writing very slowly in capital letters, using a hopeless broken biro. They were like a 4-year-old's first efforts.

This evening he came down at 7.30. I was sitting reading the papers by the fire and heard him drawing back the curtains, allowing the darkness to pour in. 'Don't do that, it's still the evening. You've just had an afternoon sleep.' He looked thunderstruck when I told him the time. 'Oh God,' he said three times – as though he'd just had news of an earthquake in Bridport. His face furrowed as he thought of another long evening of TV and biscuits.

Saturday 15th December

Today's distinguished guest was Edward Montagu of Beaulieu, whom Caroline had met at an HHA meeting and asked to tea. He hadn't been to Mapperton for ages, and my father struggled to remember even his father, who had been his godfather – 'M of B', as it says on the barograph. I read him out the *Who's Who* reference to refresh both our memories. 'Baronetcy in the 1880s.' 'Well, he must be quite an old man by now.' Actually he's twenty years younger than you, and his entry is three times as long. Not that that's a lot to go by.

We had tea ready by 3.45 and I managed to get three more Christmas cards done to prevent him slipping off to bed. 'You've done it very well,' he said, showing that I was really the one behind the

Christmas cards idea, 'and now I'm going to get my hot water bottle.' But Caro was ready for him in the hall: 'I've locked your bedroom, Higgy. You've got a visitor for tea.' He wandered off upstairs nevertheless, but then came back: 'I can't get into my bedroom.' Mercifully Edward arrived and stayed about half an hour during which my father was silent. 'I don't know whether he remembers me,' he said afterwards – and nor did we. We saw him off in his Daimler – MMM 1 – but not before C had pointed out the garden, which she is persuading English Heritage (which he chairs) is heritage in its own right, and not just an appendage of the house.

Sunday 16th December

The office was in full Sunday morning flow, with Andrée and Caroline fixing up Burcombe grants and me on the floor with farm building valuations, when Dick Powell and his brother Rex arrived with our three Christmas trees. Caroline showed Dick the 18th c. Brodrepp silver chalice which Melplash Church has returned to us and he nodded, 'I used to have communion out of that!' We told him the builders would be in the vestry for a few more days and he said, 'Oh no,' just as Alice (his wife) had said yesterday, because it's getting close to church decorating day.

I had to insist on his asking transport cost for the trees. Dick asked about the shoot as he often does and I felt ashamed, as I often do, that I did not know all the details as he must think I should. After all, he made most of the gates, bridges and duck hides and planted almost all the trees for miles around. I asked him to come out one day and he said he would. He seems fully recovered.

Friday 28th December

A week of very stormy weather. The rain let up on Christmas Eve and a small band trooped up the drive to sing carols: Mima, Frances, her friend Philip Stevens, Tristan (for one carol to Shirley and Stan),

Val – sensibly with torches and a Shakespearean lantern, and me. We sang briefly to the Hodgins in the Old Rectory and collected Kirsty at the Stable before we reached the cottages. 'When a poor man came in sight' sounds yucky on these occasions. Joyce joined in, but Jim and Jo pleaded they'd 'never learn'd any carols'. Dick and Alice were pleased to part with the church silver, beautifully cleaned for the service. We ended up with a delicious mulled wine with Val and her family.

On Christmas morning Mima came down with her stocking looking miserable from lack of sleep owing to wind and rain pouring through her window. The boys did not appear at all – next year I am not wrapping any more stocking presents for them. After 20 years it is just about the worst event of the year, removing both sleep and all hope of the midnight service.

C reminds me that breakfast was appalling: we had abandoned formal Christmas breakfast for what we hoped would be more relaxed self–help, but the coffee machine broke down, the toaster went up in flames and the pepper pot emptied totally over Perceval's egg.

Church was sublime with two charming smily grandfathers, P and Pat Stacy Waddy, bunched behind the altar giving benedictions and two lovely granddaughters reading the lessons. Sylvia and my father attended. Sylvia insisted on standing for the hymns, propped up by C and the Australian girl Carolyn. Higgy sat far back but I moved him up behind me. He remembered most of his responses, even in the ASB. Val took the collection and I came out and chatted to a set of Duncan Forbes's relations and said goodbye. Then I came round the corner alarmed to find the whole congregation pouring into the house for sherry. Mulled wine and carols is one thing, but why does Caroline.... ah well.

Christmas lunch went OK, with children munching £1s and 20ps excavated from the pudding. Crackers were poor but everyone stayed cheerful, thank goodness. It is all such an effort.

Boxing Day saw at least 50 people through the house, mostly relations turning out for the family shoot. Two Indian boys, Murad (son of Geeti Ali) and Azhar (son of Zehra Tyabji – all old friends from Delhi), turned up. I led poor Murad through the driving sleet of the first drive, down the hill below Coltleigh and over the Birch Hill escarpment. We skidded along in mud, attempting to be beaters, with shots all round, feeling like bit-parts at the Somme. I felt sorry for Murad until he confessed he'd recently been to a French boar hunt.

Raymond has put a white gate at the top of the stairs, but now my father bangs loudly on it, asking to be released. 'I only want to go down to the library.' 'You can't. It's much too early and the alarm is on. Go back to bed.' 'Why can't I go downstairs?' 'Go on back to bed, it's not fair on other people, wait till 7 am.' Luckily his watch was half an hour slow but he didn't know that.

It's no joke fighting with this stubborn old man at 5 or 6 am and after every encounter we lie furious, exhausted and unable to sleep. Is he wearing us down? Is he winning? Does it matter? We have got somehow to bring his getting–up time forward to an hour which suits other people. [We hadn't, by this time, recognised that he was not just 'confused', but suffering from a form of Alzheimer's.]

The day after Boxing Day we had some friends in to a drink and he came down very confused about the time and wandered through the party. 'Who are all these people?' Later we were all about to sit down to cold meat and cheese in the kitchen when he turned up again, cross when he heard that it was still evening. However C asked him to stay and having hesitated he sat down happily to a very nice meal and was plied with presents and chocolates. He was almost affectionate, as he can be.

1991

Tuesday 1st January

Today dawned pink, mauve and yellow behind the pine trees, softly reflected on the Tudor ceiling, and I scrambled out of bed to take an inadequate photograph. Last night the children had a last-minute New Year dinner party for 16 and we have locked the mess into the dining room. I am sorry that three good glasses were broken, one of the Meissen plates was found on the floor, the Beaume-de-Venise was attacked, etc, but of course much more delighted that they have finally got it together and enjoyed themselves (an ache in my throat is ready to betray any insincerity about this which may creep in). Mima, easily the youngest, seems to have joined in well and put up with all the loutishness.

Caro and I and Carolyn, our helper, walked with Louis over the ha-ha across the field just before midnight to hear the rival church bells ringing out the New Year, the deep dong coming up the valley from Netherbury contrasting with the semi-urban peal and raucous cheering from Beaminster. We went back to join the celebrations and I had a fascinating, if hardly lucid, conversation with Bruno Kavanagh about the looming Gulf War in which he reflected a lot of concern from friends in the US who are dreading or rejecting the call-up; and about Italy.

Day after day we have wrestled with my father over the gate. Last night he actually woke us five times in the night, to which have to be added four times for Sylvia (Carolyn was having a night off). We dread the 'Blind Pew' effect of him crossing the landing to shake the gate and then tap loudly on our door, every forty minutes from about 4.30. Caro is going to sleep somewhere else tonight, and mercifully I'm in London.

Sunday 6th January (Epiphany)

I took Louis for the first drive of the shoot at Ramsmoor, struggling through strong winds. We retrieved two between us just below Bungalow (now only a heap of planks, waiting to be rebuilt for the Browns). His was a 'dead' hen pheasant in a hedge, the subject of much speculation because a hen had been winged but had gone down the hedge the other way – the guns looked suspiciously at Louis. Mine which flew even higher was General Howlett's peak cap, caught high in the top hedge just out of reach. He was flushed with walking and as always in very good humour. I went round and just managed to fish it out with a stick, feeling like a good little soldier. I was told later that day that not long ago he had been commanding the whole Army of the Rhine.

With a fair amount of cajoling my father wrote a letter to his younger sister yesterday:

Darling Betts

*Thank you so much for the Television set which you have so kindly rented for me for Christmas. I am going to try it out in my bedroom on days when I get up very early. We are having a very stormy week. * We are looking forward to the spring and your next visit. Much love,*

Hinch

*In more ways than one. This morning he was up at 5.45 a.m. rattling the gate. I lectured him and hustled him back and turned on the new TV and we tried to go back to sleep but he stalked round the house as usual, searching for an exit, and then returned to negotiate the gate. I stood by the door listening, then came slowly out to find he had simply dropped a leather pouffe over the gate and used it to climb over! He was already halfway downstairs, sneaking into the library, muttering when he saw me that he had to go and see to his 'papers'. I decided this one wasn't worth winning but we then lay awake for another hour vowing to get him into a home or lock him into his room or both if necessary. Finally in search of peace I turned to Anita Desai's book about an old persecuted Bombay refugee called Baumgartner with whom my father seems to have quite a bit in common.

Saturday 19th January

As I write he is prowling round the house looking for a bed. We now have a 'rule' that he goes to bed no earlier than 4 p.m., and it is now just 3. We have locked his door but yesterday this didn't stop him getting fully clothed into the bed in the Tudor room. We left him until late and then frog-marched him out of bed and down the corridor, into his pyjamas and into his own bed. 'Leave me alone, I'm all right in this bed, I'm not harming anyone, leave me alone!' I was mentally exhausted afterwards, but we have to do it, it's our house too — we have to live normally.

The time has now arrived for us to move him out, temporarily, so that at least the 'carers' can get some rest and we can sleep at night. We have even had to move from our own room to the chapel room to get out of earshot. What with the cat, also in his dotage, stalking round looking for a good room to kip or pee in, we are all turning into nomads.

The Gulf War is in its third day, but most of the emotional energy this week has gone into phone calls around the family, with three out of four sisters wavering over the decision to move him. There is no point in recording who was the most upset, when or why: what hits us is the rebound whereby the two of us feel we have to carry everyone else's agony. This sounds presumptuous but it is fact. Our telephone voices get lower and lower until we find we are dragging each other down, regardless of the cause of the problem. Why should a silly old man have this kind of hold over his children in what is already turning into his after-life? In my position all I can do is to hold the line and tug, i.e. make gradual decisions and hope that everyone will fall in behind in the end. But it has strained us to the limit.

There are much brighter things to record, such as the lemon-coloured light as I came into the office this morning; the misty views towards Loscombe and Poorton; the speed and colour of plump pheasants flying down into Holeacre; the silhouettes of the yew hedges in strong sunlight; the cheerful, redoubtable faces of Alice and Joyce outside the old school; Martin, the carpenter's expression yesterday as he was refixing Jemima's attic window against strong wind and rain, knowing that his wife was dying at home – these are some of the highlights of Mapperton in winter which put an old man's dementia into very deep shade.

Saturday 26ᵗʰ January

A haggard figure stumbles along outside the kitchen as we are catching up with the Gulf news: 'Is there any marmalade?' For some reason I warm to the apparition – it is such a wonderful, time-honoured question and the plain fact is that after taking a lot of care setting his breakfast tray I have left out the one essential. 'Of course you must have some marmalade.' I found half a spoonful in a pot, but when Shirley appeared with a new jar he beamed and turned back to the library.

This was decision week for both the old gentlemen. Our distinguished 17-year-old (cat) Sukie finally gave up the ghost at the vet on Tuesday and we all miss him terribly – I have tried to trace his relations outside Huntingdon but without success.

We had the normal disturbed night in the 'chapel' room. I got up as usual at 7.30 but there was no sound from my father's room and I wondered, not for the first time, if his final moment had come too. I remember feeling completely calm about it and hoping this was how I would really feel when the moment came. I went downstairs and opened the shutters, wondering what could have kept him in bed — at least this would help the nursing home, was my attitude. Then I heard the familiar radio sound and went down to make breakfast.

Yesterday he showed his familiar patrician impatience which removes my lingering doubts about moving him. We went for a short outing in the car. 'Do we have to take that dog?' Of course we're taking Louis. I drove him silently up the hill, saying I only had a quarter of an hour before a meeting at Hooke, and he yelped in alarm as I turned off the main road. 'But I don't want to go that way, I want to go down to Beaminster and up the tunnel road.' He gestured vaguely with his hand. 'I'm sorry, but I don't have much time,' I said, barely even enjoying the answering back. 'We are going up the hill to Coltleigh.' And so we did, but he moaned at the cold and the landscape and refused to recognise George Brown at the farmhouse. I now also see in others' faces that my father no longer exists for them — and how could he? After giving Louis a quick walk with borrowed time I drove him back, with some relief, into the garage, glad to get off to the meeting at Hooke. A rescue plan for the school has begun.

Saturday 2ⁿᵈ February

Well, in the end we took him away. I deliberately said nothing to him in advance because of the endless uncertainty in his mind. Earlier in the day, and aware of the heavy irony, I had once or twice suggested an 'afternoon drive' in the car but he complained, quite reasonably, that the weather was unsuitable. It was a dismal, cold, grey day. Julia and Tim were staying, and we had a final Sunday lunch *en famille*, I have to say more cheerful than usual because of our expectations of the day — a bit like the courage of soldiers when war finally breaks out. I can't help these strong metaphors because feelings can be quite powerful.

I took him some coffee in the sitting room, hoping he would stay in range but he soon began to wander off to the library. I went crossly in pursuit and started the attack. I told him Peter Claydon, our doctor friend, had asked him out to tea and we were setting off right away. I remember his wary, anxious look but it was free of suspicion. Then he began to dig in like the Iraqi infantry, and who could blame him? Could he tell? 'I'm not going out today.' 'Yes you are, Peter asked us, you've got to come.' 'No, I don't want to.' I decided against a forced march and so went in search of troops, and luckily at this point Orlando offered himself. I followed him in with Caroline and Shirley moments later and to my great relief he had already cajoled him on to his feet, so that we only had to guide him out to the car – tottering like a sacrificial ram.

Mile after mile he asked where we were going. Mile after mile we made up answers like the witches in fairy tales, coaxing the children deeper into the wilderness. Just a little further, the other side of Dorchester, near Wimborne, not far now, just outside Ringwood, until we drew up outside Fritham House, the New Forest Nursing Home.

I am not going to describe our arrival, or the sequel, except to say that every night this week he has tried to get up in the night, pack his bags in the morning and go to bed in the afternoon. Apparently he visited an elderly widow who told him he shouldn't be in her bedroom at night but that he could come in during the day, which he regularly does. All this will be amusing to read in the future, but for now we are having a rest – he has disturbed us for too long and the nurses must take care of him.

Sunday 17th February

We have had a relaxed three weeks, enjoying being in the house by ourselves, knowing that my father was safely tucked into the New Forest. But already the old tension had crept back as we prepared for his return this afternoon. I drove over to fetch him. The nurses seemed quite happy with him, and of course we forget they are so used to the elderly confused. Apparently he has been packing his suitcases day after day, carrying them downstairs thinking he is on some foreign holiday and about to be collected. Even when the nurses remove the suitcases from the hall he carries his things down in piles, saying that he is 'leaving the hotel today'. One lot he even put in the back of someone's car.

The fire has been lit in the hall/sitting room and the house smells very sweet. Caroline has brought plants in. There's been a lot of spring-cleaning, the library ceiling has been painted and furniture polished. The naval sofa has been smartly restored and fits well with the Egyptian suite in the drawing room. A radiator burst above the dining–room, so that room is now drying out and warm.

'Do they know I am coming?' he asked in the car. But he will never understand that nowadays none of this is in his honour, the very opposite: all of it has only been possible because of his absence. The house goes on at its own pace, he goes away, the two are not and should not be interdependent. It's just that we have hardly ever seen them apart.

Last night C and I decided to get at the cellar, and we went down for an hour and created a dust storm. I swept and reoccupied the barrel-shaped room with the old practice tennis wall while Caroline and Henry, the Beaminster vacuum cleaner, sucked up the worst dust. I opened a rusty window and cold fresh air roared in – for the first time in years.

I drove him home at about 5.40 pm, racing past Rampisham across Toller Down. He walked uncertainly down the path to the front door and then sat in his coat by the fire, saying it was strange to be back. His internal clock seems to have improved, but for how long? From outside we watched him climbing up to draw his bedroom curtains. Then a new night nurse called Jane came and he went happily to bed.

Later we heard the sad news that Joan Best's house at Hincknowle had a chimney fire this afternoon and almost burnt to the ground.

No one was hurt, but there was a desperate rescue operation to get most of the furniture out of the ground floor. For us it was a terrible reminder of the risks of looking after old country houses.

Sunday 24th February

The fox has got one of the bantam chickens this week, and is apparently reproducing himself, judging by howls at night across the valley. He was allowed to stray into the Newalls' pig field to pick up placentas but managed to swallow some new piglets too.

My father has made his first, rather comic, appearance on the answerphone. A London female voice asked if he had a photograph of the gardens for a magazine and his reply after heavy breathing was: 'Well it's Mr Montagu speaking. I'm rather bad with a camera these days, I used to be as a boy rather efficient, but I'm not doing it now, if you'd like to come up and commission somebody yourself I'd be delighted.' Well, she said, that's very kind of you but what we really wonder is whether you have a photograph of the gardens? Long pause and heavy breathing. 'No.'

This morning I woke early in spite of a late night celebrating Marzia's birthday at Sturminster Newton. I knew my father was getting up and the night nurse might not know all the ropes. Luckily all was well and I went back to listen to news of the Kuwait ground offensive which has just begun. The political hawks are on the loose, even among the bishops. Downstairs I let the dog out and began to make myself some toast, but my father came into the kitchen – crossing a minefield in clearly demarcated hostile territory – for a chat and I had to divert him back to the library. 'Who else is here, the family? That's very good news. Do you want some breakfast? Well there's a nice girl who's just gone, or you could try Mrs Clark.' Thank you so much, why don't you just get back to your TV set and stay there.

Saturday 2nd March

It was the weekend of the owl. Major Lewis, the expert, came over from Warminster, 'plus wife plus dog, part of team' and very smart ladders, and was joined by Val, George Brown, William Wilkinson (he was head of the Nature Conservancy Council which became English Nature) and Alistair Best who were both staying. As a first stage, owl boxes – one made by Raymond and marked 'WOL REPOS' by Mima much to Alistair's disapproval – were carefully placed in the south stable and up an ash tree on the hill. Then a four-wheel drive party set off into wind and rain to search outlying buildings between Coltleigh and Mythe. William, who is very blind but sees in a straight line, came home to the fire and we chatted happily about Eton while Kate Wilkinson and Caroline were in Bridport. The day was completed with a Hardy outing to Dorchester with Alice and Mima, who had a minor confrontation with a lamp-post.

My father is obviously reverting to old ways with biscuits and night wanderings, but manages not to irritate too much.

Saturday 9th March

I brought the Volvo back last night with a Comic Relief red nose tied to the grill, a new gear lever and an overhauled gearbox, and this morning found my father almost skipping with delight to see it back, asking for the keys, impatient to go out in it an hour before time. I shook my head for a bit, but eventually agreed to walk out into the drizzle with him to look at it. He asked about the mini-wipers on the headlights, thought hard and then asked if when you turned on the lights the nose also gleamed.

Sunday 17th March

Betts is here for the weekend, and brother and sister have been sitting uncertainly together in the drawing room until they run out of things to say. This morning there was a TV programme on Hinchingbrooke

School, but at the critical moment my father started fiddling with the control and we lost vision. By the time we got it back there was nothing but talking heads at meetings and I tried in vain to interest the audience. At one moment my father leaned forward and saw the title 'Hinchingbrooke School' and said 'Ah, that's very exciting', but we searched in vain for views out of the oak room window to bring back memories. They exchanged a few words about the number of gardeners, and that was it.

Orlando and I were in fits before lunch yesterday (shades of Mum, Timothy (my uncle), and Betts giggling about Grandpa a generation back) when we were helping Betts and Higgy to do something for Mum's 75th birthday. Betts had it pretty well worked out and was prompting Higgy to write a few words to Mum to go with the fossil soap. 'Think of you often.' 'Long and loving relationship.' He wrote dutifully, then surprised us all by adding: *'I wish that circumstances had changed themselves'*. Even Orlando, who can't know a lot about their relationship, was quite moved by this.

He sometimes confuses names and faces so much that we cannot conduct any conversation, and this is when I wonder if we should be looking after him at all. 'Who is that person?' (His daughter, wife, sister? Mrs Clarke?) Does it matter knowing who it is, so long as I say the right thing, seems to be the argument, but I wonder if everyday life at home is worth living when you no longer know who is with you.

Rainwater is pouring through the gardens, overfilling the pools, and dampening spirits. We walked along the lynchets to Mythe yesterday to mark out a proposed new plantation. Orlando and his dog happily joined in as this affects the shooting. At last we have agreed on the new letter to send to the guns.

Passion Sunday, and I must say I am looking forward to Easter.

Monday 1st April

I told Perceval his car was missing this morning – quite an effective April Fool because Orlando just might have borrowed it for a party, or he might have thought so. Thirteen little lambs are dancing about in the orchard on legs like pipe cleaners, but sadly one triplet has died and the ewe is sick. Roy came up with a pen yesterday full of bantams and ducklings to replace Mr Fox's recent Mapperton dinners. We all stood in the sun delighted as he unloaded them. The pot shop opened and the first spring visitors are braving the wind: at least Stan is keeping warm inside with a stove, and is earning some commissions.

I took Higgy down to Loscombe today to see the Andrewes' garden – some of it planted with his help. It was a chilly grey day and after seeing the daffs we warmed up with sherry. Perceval (who married them) joined us and we had a very amusing teasing chat, my father putting on a party smile. He attended both Easter services. On Sunday I sang the Easter responses – not too loud I hope. Philip Youngman, an ex-Plymouth Brother in Melplash, said not to read music, played the familiar hymns and P gave us a superb new version of his Monica Furlong sermon on the necessity of doubt. Later he and I walked round the European stained glass using Dr Cole's notes.

I had tried to ease up on Easter eggs but Mima – now more mobile and nearing her driving test – went down to Beaminster and made up for it and in the end we all had at least two each. Sylvia has nibbled at hers but has not been feeling too well, mostly tucked on to the sitting room sofa.

We are closing on a deal with the National Maritime Museum over the 4th Earl's official papers which should provide enough capital for farmhouse conversions and maintenance – and may even pay us back a few train fares.

Saturday 6th April

I met Timmy and his bicycle on Salisbury station and came on down. The mother of triplets is very unwell and has come into the outhouse. We fed the lambs which seem frisky enough but the vet thinks there may be a fourth one inside. Shirley is now of course the foster mother.

My father has been giving the nurses a little more sleep but there is another battle going on for his bedroom key. (C adds): 'Yesterday afternoon Hinch was wandering round the house with keys from the dining room, central hall, drawing room, angrily thrusting them into his bedroom door and trying to force it open. I got the keys back to their proper doors but not my father-in-law into a reasonable frame of mind. He finally told Stan he didn't care and would sleep in the library.'

Then today I had twenty minutes of little boy's furrowed brow and minimal knowledge of human rights, armoured with logic-chopping developed by a political warhorse. 'I want to know who has locked the door of my room. I don't see why the owner of a room should not be allowed the key. I might want to put on some clothes, or collect something upstairs.'

'All the evidence,' I said, 'suggests that you will do none of those things. What you actually do, and have done frequently, is to go upstairs to bed in the middle of the afternoon, before tea. Then you get up at 4 or 5 the next morning and wake the whole house up.' He spluttered, and the full force of the Tory smoking room snarl came out. 'You mean I go into ladies' bedrooms and roger them?' Then, indignantly and haughtily: 'I never go to bed before tea.'

We had a sweepstake for the Grand National and fourteen of us, including Gemma and Richard Ollard who was visiting, put £1 into the pool. Sickeningly Gwendoline's horse, the favourite, was overtaken in the last few minutes by Seagram – the horse my father had picked out of only two offered him. C and I exchanged looks of doom, regarding him as the least deserving winner. However it kept him downstairs a bit longer. All my earlier arguments were proved (if they had to be) the next morning when he woke at 7, after the new night nurse had already left.

Sunday 7th April

We were awake at 5, worrying about the nurse setting off the alarm. Finally I got up to make his breakfast, and took Louis outside.

He seemed blind to the pheasant strutting past the gate. We trotted round the church. It was one of those lovely clear sunny mornings which make you long for more life. The nurse drove off in her car. There was a strong smell of the fox but the ducks were shut in and the bantams looked fairly cocky. A couple of deer browsing below the pools moved off. I crunched the gravel, half hoping Caroline would hear and look out. Then back to the front door. Of course he had locked it. A minute later I spotted him tugging at a curtain and tapped on the window. 'You've locked us out!' 'Oh sorry,' he said, but somehow, even when he is most innocent, I still suspect him of evil designs, as if he were always acting one of Alec Guinness's cronies in *The Ladykillers*.

The same afternoon Stan suddenly died – Shirley Clark's husband, aged only 65. He had been a storeman at Numatic and retired at Mapperton. He had his own mind and a lot of experience overseas. Stan was a bit shy of us at first but after five years had become both an essential support for Shirley and a growing bit part in the Mapperton pantomime. We have all been hit very hard. Fortunately the family has rallied around Shirley ever since.

At the same time a ewe died after producing twins. The coroner's policeman dropped in earlier, said he'd been a sheep farmer in Scotland, and helped me to lift the ewe into the sun in a wheelbarrow. Julia's Timmy (nearly 9) was staying, unperturbed throughout these dramas. He fed the lambs, minded the pot shop and led a line of small children round the yard and the bonfire.

Sunday 28th April

There is another little tearaway, in Shirley's family, who's been helping in the pot shop. You can hear him yelling round the back, shouting in the courtyard, or screaming up in the flat. He is tremendously energetic and a great help to Kirsty. Imagine this boy was also in the house, constantly walking up and down, demanding attention every few minutes – just like the old man. Eventually we would go mad or slap him or both. We would not be able to stand the sort of idiotic repetitive questioning he throws at us and to which we now have to respond. And the fuss with small things like meals and razors. Shirley's diary for this week had: 'Thursday: Up 8.30, etc... chucked lunch out of library window.'

Louis and I watched two melanistic cocks fighting in the orchard, jumping up two feet in the air and flying at each other. The pity is that I don't have the zest to fly at the other old corncrake; and it wouldn't do any good. C thinks my general development was stunted by him. I doubt that, but I certainly feel bruised and unwilling to fight. There must be better things to fight for. However genuine my affection for him has been at various times in the past, it is now pretty nominal and barely flickers. This diary is a fairly accurate thermometer.

I drove him over to Hooke this morning and he really enjoyed it, recalling the pre-1914 years. Trying to describe his feelings he said slowly when we got back to the garage: 'It makes oneself feel warm.' He has a lot of difficulty expressing words, and phrases get stuck at the back of his mouth like 'er... the things er... you pull together and er... fasten with an iron bar' (i.e. 'er... shutters.')

We've been tidying up the brambles round the tennis court, trying to enjoy our private orchard out of everyone's reach. Higgy seems to be getting more active with the warm weather, which means he pesters people more. He walked up to the main road to Kirsty's today, ploughing his way thoughtlessly through the new grass seed! We all pray it's not a precedent.

Sunday 19th May

If any more nurses say 'What a dear old man', 'he's a lovely person' or anything like that when I walk into the house they risk being garrotted. I was on duty all yesterday afternoon – admittedly watching the first half of the Cup Final when Gazza was carried off plus a good deal of *A Passage to India* – and every few minutes he either said he didn't understand the programme or complained selfishly about 'that woman — what's her name — who's got my hot water bottle and won't let me go to bed'. You can't just make the excuses of old age in this case. Madness perhaps. It's lucky I'm not in court to testify. If you leave him for a moment he darts along the passage and starts hammering on Shirley's door, shouting her name up the stairs (if he can remember it) and looking like an anguished half-starved scarecrow who ought to be on a bonfire. He is here berating one of Dorset's saintliest people who having recently lost her husband instead has to put up with one of West Dorset's foremost con-men, a man who has hidden a secret life of shame, vanity and penury behind two inches of pseudo-Father Christmas and Conservative gloss. All right, this may be well over the top, but you sometimes have to look over the top to see things in perspective.

One of the bantams came clucking round the door of the office and C and I stared, astonished at its determination. It came jerking around our area and proceeded to strut into a filing tray. Could it be... about to lay? Oh no, something else. We started to chase it away but it let out a fat white plops and scuttled out into the yard looking pleased.

It's supposed to be Higgy's 85th birthday tea today and I can hardly bear to think about it. We are having a concert in the church afterwards, not of course in his honour but he can always shuffle in for the rehearsals. His real birthday is on Wednesday and Alice Powell is going to take him in a card – which is just right; it may be his only one. [No, about ten came: it shows some people care, even now.]

I tried to explain what was happening today, saying there would be a few people coming to a birthday tea. He responded with one of those splendid pieces of waffle designed for staff and committees. 'I think we could have a meal which is not too formal, otherwise we get into not a very satisfactory situation in the dining room.' Hear hear, quite right, well said. Luckily Kate's coming over to add a touch of sanity.

Obsessions are hard to deal with. Shirley has continuously had to avoid driving him to Newman's with two razors (in perfectly good condition) and the last time she had to contradict him crossly, echoing his own ridiculous protests: 'Mr Montagu this is not your town, not your shops, and we are not going to Newman's.'

Anyhow we're going off to New Orleans, and it may not be far enough.

[It wasn't. We found one of his old cronies there, a perfectly nice girl who had stayed with him in the sixties and, of course, kept on about 'darling Hinch' and 'I haven't seen him for ages'.]

Sunday 16th June

We got back from two glorious weeks in New York, New Orleans and North Carolina last week. I had been praying daily that we would get that holiday in before... well, before some terrible event occurred to prevent it... and we have. The only telephone calls were from the children, who actually seemed to miss us.

I came down early on Thursday to talk to two Hooke teachers about a possible fund-raising campaign for the school. We sat beside the loggia with beers in warm sun and I felt wonderful.

Back down to earth. I told the old man I was going to shave the whiskers on his neck. He looked doubtful.

'What are you going to do...? You might cut my throat, and then before long I'll be in Brampton graveyard...' I declined to comment. The fact is that I am the one who deserves the medal for endurance, especially for shaving the old cockerel.

While on this subject, sadly more chickens have been taken by Mr Fox, and we have been ticked off by the vet for not looking after the sheep properly (flies and ticks). We now realise this is because Stan's knowledge was always there to help Shirley. Yesterday a phone call from Ethel Way told us a lamb was on the way out, so George went and finished her off.

Sunday 23rd June

Last night we took Anne Marris out to dinner with the Talbots – the nearest thing to Claridges around here. I asked my father if he had a message for Elizabeth (formerly Durlacher) and he said: 'Yes, a message of recollection and thanks for what we did in the old days when we met.' At dinner she looked a bit surprised, and listened to me patiently as I told her what a Hinch-centred life he had had, despite the appearances and his kindliness. I said he never met anyone on equal terms and always preferred people to come up to him, as it were, in his eyrie. He had painted himself into a corner politically. She sounded interested and not unbelieving, but said that I was probably too close to be a judge.

A phrase from Pam Fooks, who listened to one of my moans this weekend, stays with me: 'Well John, you have to look after him while he's there.' I am amazed how many nice people like Pam remember him with affection, even if I know they have never lived with him. They see him through tinted glass. Of course he had good qualities, but I keep wanting to tell people the whole truth. Maybe the truth isn't good for them and they would rather not know it. Maybe half the truth is all anyone ever knows.

I started the day feeling very depressed. This may be to do with the farm insurance which is driving me potty, but getting the old man's bacon and egg comes into it somewhere. The rain is pouring heavily down, overfilling the reservoirs at last.

Monday 15th July

Caroline adds:

A truly appalling day at Mapperton.

1. Our good friend and secretary, Andrée, came into the kitchen, eyes blotchy and red, sniffing and not meeting my gaze. Reason: yesterday afternoon I walked out to the back

of the house and found her and her eight-year-old daughter handing over the two family guinea pigs for Shirley to look after while they are on holiday. Instead of saying how lovely – which I would have if I'd had a minute's warning – I exclaimed, gut feelings to the fore, 'Oh, no, not guinea pigs as well to look after; anyway they'll probably be eaten by the foxes and we've two cats coming on Friday.'

Tears from Leonie all night, tears from Andrée. And it is her last working morning at Mapperton for two months as she is going to stay with her parents in France.

2. When as usual Shirley came to lock Hinch's bedroom door at two o'clock, the key, last used by his Consultus girl, Fiona, was not in the right place. Nor could we find it anywhere, nor could I find Fiona on the telephone.

3. Meanwhile the Painswick Horticultural Society was bringing a group round the house and garden. I presented the invoice to the organizer who said, 'Oh no.' I'd done the invoices figures quite wrong, depriving the estate of half the money. So back into the church to go through to the house and ...

4. Hinch had locked Valerie and me into the church. Luckily we could still go out the other door.

5. I realised this signalled he'd gone to bed and, true to form, there he was at 3.45 tucked into bed with his nightcap on. So I ruthlessly drew back the curtains and the blinds and spitting like an alley cat told him it was far too early etc. etc. His smug response – 'As soon as you've gone out of the room I shall get up and draw them again' – drew another stream of articulate irascibility.

6. My mother, now at 4.15 dressed and ready to come downstairs, took on a fit of the blues and tearful for the next hour or so said she wished she'd done more for me,

she felt guilty, she hadn't tried hard enough and hadn't tried hard enough to keep going, she must do more and felt full of regrets, and wished she'd had lots of children to play with each other. That she finds it difficult actually to speak made it all the more painful and each of these sadnesses she repeated at least three or four times.

7. Luke lost his wallet.

Sunday 28th July

This last week has been especially tiresome because Shirley has been off (therefore VM as well), although Erika from Queensland has been a wonderful help. Meanwhile I was able to enjoy the Monteverdi *Vespers* in the Albert Hall and Rachel Scott's dinner party back in Dorset. I spent most of Thursday night with Sylvia. She was very heavy to lift and 'full' like summer wine.

I drove my father down to the square and back and he was quite cheerful. 'Do you ever go up there?' he asked as we passed the Coltleigh turning, so we drove up the hill, and parked outside the bungalow site to gaze at the view. I often test his memory of farms we can see up there and he got about one out of four, but the sheep house at Loscombe is hard to make out. The sea was a good colour and he asked what the yellow cliff was and I said Golden Cap and he said, 'Oh yes', unconvincingly. I noted George and Bobbie have a new letter box on the gate here 400 yards from home, showing that they are looking forward to the new house we are building on the site of the old bungalow. Aren't we all? But we are still waiting for DCC building regs. Meanwhile Burcombe farmhouse awaits its turn.

I tested him again this morning – this time on heraldry, with a copy of Burke's on my knee. 'And so where were the Montagus before they went to Northants?' I asked. He said 'Hooke' – with some truth because the Paulets had lived there in the 1560s. The answer I wanted was Somerset and I tried to labour the point about the Norman

Montagus' link with Shepton Montague near Wincanton. He lost concentration, so I turned to the coat of arms with its fine supporters. I noticed for the first time that the triton had an eastern crown. I then mentioned the eagle and he suddenly started quoting the heraldry by heart, fesse gules, etc., his memory presumably going back to house tours at Hinchingbrooke. When he got to 'eagle vert depressed' I was quite amused but think he meant 'displayed'. This particular 'eagle depressed' seems likely to run and run, though perhaps not fly. He is certainly in excellent shape, unlike those around him. Can we physically stand it for another two, five or perhaps more years? [*C notes*: Ten?] At any rate he is going back to his 'hotel' in the New Forest in a month or so to give us all a summer break.

He received a letter from [our US cousins] the Kneens this month mentioning our visit to them – he said it was 'very complimentary'.

I have found two notes in my diary:

Finding an empty honesty-box during his walk one afternoon my father asked, rather crossly: 'Do they think my money is going to be sent to the King or Queen, or whoever we've got?'

Another day, during a drive in the car, he suddenly said: 'Thank you very much for taking charge of all this – I don't want to go through it all again.'

When I remember this, it sounds rather moving.

Sunday 18th August

We are just back in London after a week's sailing in the Isle of Wight, and I thought I would dial 441 to see if he was all right. 'Who is it?' said a strained old voice with great effort. 'John.' 'John who? Oh, John.' 'How's the weather down there?' 'We're having very nice weather, much regretting your absence. When are you coming down?' I told him we'd been in the IOW and he asked if Dick Peto was there. I said no [not for 25 years], but we'd been playing under 10s cricket on Dick's old grass court. He sounded amused and said, 'That's very good', and rang off.

Wednesday 21ˢᵗ August

A new landmark today when C returns to Dorset and is faced with the old oppression and the whole panoply of old-age caring. His time is up, neither she nor I nor others around us can stand it. We feel like Yeltsin on a Mapperton tank. It seems so obvious to us now that we cannot occupy the same ground as my father any longer. The pressure is mainly psychological and it has diminished our life intolerably.

Friday 23ʳᵈ August

Last night and this morning I have had conversations with various members of the family and feel exhausted even by 9.30 a.m. Some are inconclusive and I cannot understand why we are not getting the fullest support [mainly not from Anne and Julia] but I think everyone will realise the situation in the end.

Sunday 25ᵗʰ August

I was in the office just settling down to write when I heard a scraping by Shirley's door, and went out to find a familiar worried creased face turned up at me. My father. 'She's out,' I said, 'there's no one there. Is there anything you want?' I knew the answer perfectly well and started mouthing it: 'The key to my bedroom.'

'Not till five o'clock. Don't you remember...(etc.) The best thing would be for you to go back to the library, unless you want a walk... Is there anything you want?'

'I don't want a walk, I'm hoping something is going to happen.' Then with emphasis: 'A cup of tea and a piece of cake.' Epic, I thought.

'Certainly, you want a cup of tea, and a piece of cake. I'll bring it along right away,' I said, but I didn't. I sat down again and then a young sophisticated garden visitor suddenly said loudly through the office door: 'Is that a bell? Can you tell me what it was for?' It is like a school bell, high up on the kitchen wall and controlled by a long wire. I told her it was probably a tea bell for people working in the garden. Minutes later another woman came out of the outside 'Rocket' loo and I heard: 'I haven't seen one of those since I was a child – and look at that bell!' So now I have shut the door on them all. Such are the joys of a Bank Holiday.

Saturday 31st August

We have had a very difficult week, with numerous hours spent on the telephone explaining to the family what we think should happen. The decision cannot easily be shared because it is really our problem – but there is a lot of feeling that it is all happening too quickly and people haven't had time to join in the decision. This is where participatory decision-making becomes a painful nightmare, as if you are slowly peeling a plaster off a deep wound, unkind to all around you.

The fact is that an elderly person with severe dementia, probably Alzheimer's – needs residential care which cannot be provided here. He doesn't have to be treated as though he is dying, as some members of the family seem to imagine. But of course all this is compounded by their vision of continuity – you can't enjoy change unless you are controlling it – and some distrust of our intentions. Given his attitude to me in the past, they can't be blamed for this, and yet I protest that the attention at this stage should be given to the carers around him too. We are all exhausted, and we are not giving him or ourselves freedom to live naturally. I also want to anticipate what can only become more painful for all of us in time. Both the doctors involved support this view.

In a week's time I am driving him to the New Forest again (good metaphor for an old tree-lover?), and after that we will make the long–term decision which has only been taken in principle. I went into the library just now and decided to broach the subject very gently – well, is there an honourable way to do it when someone is demented? I'm now fairly certain there isn't.

'I've spoken to Peter Claydon and you're booked in to the clinic in a week's time – New Forest, for a check–up, Dr Claydon,' I repeated, trying to get the key words all in together. 'Claydon, who's that? I don't know him, I haven't received any letter about it. Why don't you go instead, they would much prefer a younger chap than someone preaching on at them,' he said, bridling in a brilliant, cruelly ironic echo of an old political meeting. I pressed on, amazed at him. 'It's a check–up, I can't go instead of you. Peter Claydon is meeting you there, and Kate is coming…' He blinked at me and for a moment we stared suspiciously at each other and I wondered why I still wondered if he had seen through it all, seen it was a frame-up. Later when I said, 'Kate' for tea he heard 'cake' and I said, yes.

Sunday 8th September

This is dawn on the last day. I woke up at 5 and dreamed I was in an Indian pony cart, stopping somewhere on the road to Delhi, when I got a phone call from Kate worrying about yet another relation, sick or elderly. Moral: you can never altogether get away. I should have learned that long ago. I was reminded of a gunfight in a Czech cartoon I saw years ago in which the cowboys shoot each other to pieces until there are only hands left holding the smoking guns, and then they are blown away too. Caroline also had anxiety dreams about Higgy and didn't at all mind being woken from them at 6 a.m.

Today we really are driving him into the New Forest, and here is another image from a film – a Japanese courtly one in which the elderly are all eventually driven up the road to the mountain where they sit on a bench and silently expire in the snow. I am still not sure if this practice continues anywhere. Perhaps among the Ainus of Hokkaido? It is the very opposite of the Dogon principle of glorifying death and letting off Kalashnikovs. Then there is all the 17th century English background. He may be leaving the manor but at least he is going to live, or hide, in a royal deer forest. 'When did you last see your father?' Answer: Walking in the direction of Cadnam in search of chocolate gold bars.

The morning started well when Jane, the night nurse, said: 'He's been a real pain this morning, Mr Montagu has. He kept saying he wouldn't have a bath.' I was so grateful to her as I'd been expecting her to say something 'nice' to fuel the guilt machine. In fact the nurse waiting at the New Forest home, presumably hearing my strained tone, has already been giving me gentle therapy on the telephone. I now firmly believe, as Caro mostly does, that we are actually doing the right thing for him. We certainly are for us, we've had *enough!*

He looks exactly like the 'Bear That Wasn't' in the story, who came out of his cave looking lost and said, 'I'm just a man who needs a shave and wears a fur coat'. He shambles along the passage with his empty breakfast tray and stares vacantly at each of us in turn and mouths an all-too-familiar sentence. We know it all, we have heard it so many times, we answer it or ignore it before he can finish. This place is no longer good for him and it can be living hell for us.

I told him on the last journey up from Beaminster (I am trying not to be too self-conscious, but it's hard) that he was going 'to tea' and 'to stay' with Peter Claydon. This morning he told Jane that he 'wasn't going anywhere'. When I reminded him again today he said affably, 'Then I'll need to pack a bag,' and I was able to say delightedly, 'All done for you.' In fact Shirley has packed two thick brown leather suitcases for him, stuffed with corduroys and winter shirts. He'll have his clock and his photographs. I am trying to decide whether it is appropriate for him to take photos of homes he has had to leave, and I don't see why not.

Sad as it may seem that he has to go, we are also looking forward to living in the house and using it like any other family. We have already been upstairs this morning to 'close the wards', carrying out commodes and equipment from his and Sylvia's bedroom and remaking the beds. We have asked several people to stay next weekend for the Courtyard Fair. There is something very cathartic in the air. I must go and have a swim.

Coda from Caroline: I have no doubt it is the right thing for us but I find it very painful. I am haunted – as I am each time I remove my mother from Sussex to come down here, when I know she would rather stay with Perceval – by the Old Testament phase 'And the old shall go whither they wilt not.' But I now understand that this phrase is not a heart-wringer but an expression of life's inexorable flow.

Friday 27ᵗʰ September

Yesterday we had the family meeting. In a leafy suburb near Slough, in Julia's house, the future of Victor Montagu, 85 years old, the former MP, gardener and landowner, aka Viscount Hinchingbrooke, was debated by five siblings and, for the very first time in their lives, decided upon. It took over four hours. He is to remain in the New Forest nursing home unless, by December, there are any good reasons for removing him somewhere else.

Who is to speak for him? Or has he had all his say? I am alone in the view that he himself no longer has the right to any opinion about his future. I regard him as a child who cannot speak for himself – but in his case will never do so again. Having been at one time closest to him, I am now the most distant. I desperately need to be separate, perhaps until the end of his life. The others have at last recognised this, although there has been a terrible underlying assumption that we can all cope, whatever the cost.

For the last few weeks C and I have hardly been able to work, to answer letters or even to sleep properly. The lack of support at the centre of the family has been like a deadweight, however balanced by friends and others around us – especially Orlando and Mima who have given us the strongest encouragement. Why has this support failed? The answer is now coming out bit by bit, and has to do with my father's relations with each individual. There is no single reason, and there are no alliances such as I sometimes subconsciously fear.

To understand it you have to think of each different life and how it overlapped with his. The resulting picture is more like a graph with dips and curves and shaded areas. Some enjoyed brief periods with him, and then ceased to have any interest in him or developed their own lives apart. Others had a warm but perhaps superficial relationship. Some were hurt, others feel no bitterness at all. He took up with some and ignored others, all at different times and often as it suited him and not them.

No relationship with him has been completed. There remain memories to be cleared up and feelings to be expressed. Does anyone say a final goodbye to their parent? I still have a lot to sort out with him, but I have stopped trying to communicate now. But I am alone in thinking this as well. No one else seems to be able to see the futility of it.

They will all go and visit him in turn, trying to gauge his words, his attitudes, his feelings towards them. He has had that kind of hold over us in the past, but as far as I am concerned, he never will again.

<u>A draft obituary</u> – sometime in early October.
[It seems harsh, in retrospect.]

HINCH was one of those who needed other people, especially those close to him, to flatter him and get him to where he wanted. If necessary he climbed on them and rose at their expense. He was the smiling, charming Conservative MP in a green suit with a buttonhole, the family man who used or needed others for his own ends. He once certainly held liberal views – too liberal in some respects – and early in his career he was concerned enough to shape the nature and direction of the post-war State. But his politics were an expression of his strong belief in the individual. His main motivation was his own comfort and everything which improved his personal position.

Some of his family and friends might protest that he was a generous man. He was. He considered other people and gave presents to them. But they have to consider his position too. His family formed a part of his personal environment. He was an affectionate parent and enjoyed children's games; he had a sense of humour and an understanding of children. But his children had to belong to his world, they had to comply and see his point of view. Above all he had to be the centre of attention. He was used to that. It was important for constituents and fellow MPs to look up to him. He was a minor centre of influence and he enjoyed speaking from an entrenched position surrounded by admirers.

Politically he was the dark horse that never came home. He stood apart from the mainstream and was once described by *Newsweek* as 'pink and aloof'. His aristocratic manner and background helped to justify any eccentricity. In Parliament he spoke fluently and with a shrewd knowledge of the parliamentary system. He was respected for his views although few shared them. He lived life to the fullest extent, holding dinner parties for his friends regularly until Suez and the last years of the Macmillan era when his family life collapsed, my mother left him, he had to leave his old home and his career suddenly faded round him.

It was one of his remarkable talents – perhaps developed by a nurse called Scottish who 'protected' his mother from her children when she was ill – that he never revealed his feelings about himself. He never showed that he resented isolation or others' neglect. He was vain but apparently modest and always diverted compliments. He was the true loner – the statue in the middle of the pond who has convinced himself that he will always be alone.

Sunday 20th October

Could this be the last moan – or a sigh, perhaps? Do moans die away as they are replaced by sighs of joy?

Of course not. Who could live in an old Dorset manor without hearing or feeling a cold wind, creaks of floorboards and rattles of ill-fitting doors, and worst of all by far, the gloom of rainy-day solitude, and the resulting anxiety. Clocks tick – but only if we wind them up. Cats and mice scamper – but only if they are fed. Perhaps this busy atmosphere of live and dead spirits, not all unfriendly, is what people mean by ghosts.

Humans have to come into this somewhere. Energy has to be found and burned up and found again. The house will not hum by itself: it will only moan and decay. We have to occupy it. At present we only appear to.

With my father out of the way (oh yes – but quite comfortable) there are some signs of warm October air blowing through. The main one is Caroline, who comes in like the fair weather girl, smiling through the back door as soon as the rain man glides out the front [*rubbish*, she says]. This is her month [rubbish]. Like the queen on the chessboard she has done the most symbolic thing of all and captured his four-poster bed with the old French brocade. Now at last we enjoy the space, if not yet the comfort. We wander through all the rooms, wondering how to improve or change them because change them we must. Gradually. Pictures, furniture, colour and light.

Outside the countryside is constant. The white pigeons, autumn leaves, the last straggling garden visitor.

Last Sunday Orlando organised a chef and team from an Exeter hotel and they took over the kitchen from 9 a.m., providing a superbly cooked and designed meal for 17 round the dining room table. It was a sunny, windy day and some friends from Somerset came early to play crocquet on the lawn. A relaxed, happy occasion which confirms that normal life has begun again.

Sunday 3rd November

I try to allow feelings to soak through me so that I can analyse them. Don't ask where this half-baked technique comes from: it doesn't necessarily work. I don't find it easy to look forward to the next six months of 'freedom'. Do I miss him? (someone asked me this yesterday). Yes, I miss the drives up the hill and conversations we had. I miss his presence in the house, however illogical that now seems. He provided a veil of security, a sense of continuity. Of course, I know that these are all ghosts to be driven away, or at least cobwebs to be brushed off lightly. It will take time. Luckily most ghosts know they have overstayed and keep their distance.

We have moved a big sofa into the library, and Raymond and Martin have shifted two bookcases to the muniment room. It's a bit like storming the citadel, but a great improvement. The library looks empty, but we are planning to make it cosier. It needs more furniture and a fire. We tried lighting one on Friday but it ended in thick smoke and tears and the smoke alarm wailing up above. Roy needs to get up there again and stuff a few more jackdaws in his pocket.

Sunday 1st December

I went to see him at Fritham House on Friday. I drove up to his window and then backed off in case he should see me. I went in the front door and as usual found no one, until he suddenly appeared, shambling towards me with his stick and beaming a smile. He walked straight in the dining room past old ladies watching TV. Apparently he announces each day that he will be in for lunch. Then we went and sat in the library which strangely resembled the one at Mapperton. Most of our talk was about the Channel Tunnel: he said he would rather not go down it. I tried to keep the conversation off-shore but eventually he said: 'I don't know what has happened, nobody has come for me in the car. I don't drive myself, but....' Yet for the first time I wasn't seen as the driver. He is refreshingly calm about his surroundings.

1992

Saturday 22nd February

I went to see him again today. He was sitting in the day-room welcoming people to the table as though he was in Pratts. I couldn't face going in but instead got the nurse to tell him I was in the library. We had quite a pleasant 20 minutes and I tried to tell him about the house at Wherwell on the Test where his father was brought up (I've just found a headed thank-you letter from George to Uncle Hinch after he had spent a weekend at Hinchingbrooke), to make him think he was near there. I failed, of course – because he finally said he thought he was in France. Then he looked at his watch, typically, and said it was time for his lunch.

Coming down to Dorset I sometimes still look forward to a welcome, and, rightly, no longer get it. Now I shouldn't need it. This time, for instance, I had to say to myself, I don't want Shirley to say, 'Did you have a good journey?' – because we more or less live here and I would be just as irritated that she felt the need to say it. This is because my father used to drive me nearly mad with gestures of welcome, making me feel I was a visitor long after we had started coming down. And yet old memories linger….

Thursday 19th March

(From a letter to Mum in France)

> *I have just had your latest letter about your very organised life at L'Aire.*
> *Don't worry so much about possessions. I don't feel like giving you any*
> *advice because a) you've had enough of it, b) you've got too many people*
> *giving it, and c) it's only very occasionally my business anyway. Do*
> *please go on asking me specifics but don't expect much on the general.*
> *(Bitte stelle mir mal die besonderen Fragen vor, aber erwarte nicht*
> *viel von den allgemeinen.)   Not bad, but I'd have liked to get in a*
> *beziehungsweise somewhere. Ich muss do more German reading.*
>
> *As it happens we have just booked a week in the Mani in mid*
> *August — the last of the school holidays. Gai, Dan and we hope Alec are*
> *coming over. I haven't looked at the map to see where we are but we'll go*
> *and see Paddy Leigh Fermor if you send the address.*

I arrived at Mapperton without warning this evening and found
the curtains and shutters undrawn at 7.15, but Shirley said she was
about to do her round before going out to skittles. I'll mention it
again in the morning — we mustn't encourage prowlers. I asked Keith if
there was anything new and he immediately said, 'Banties — come and
see'. And perched on a rail inside the coop were no less than a dozen
bantams. Our old cockerel and his hen are sitting up in the yew tree
in the churchyard, trying not to be drawn in, but he has already had
a go at the new cock. Keith's other news was that four mallard had
appeared on the upper pond, and the lower one — due for cleaning out
on Monday — is full of toads and frogs. Kate and Nicky came to collect
Charlie, their Jacob's ram, last week, and made a very professional team.
They took nuts to attract him and Nicky simply grabbed him and sat
on his head until Kate had the trailer ready for him. Now we're waiting
for the first lambs from the ewes who came with Charlie.

Last weekend we had Jane and Ted Fawcett staying. Robin Fedden
appointed him head of marketing at the National Trust, and he is
now a lecturer in garden conservation. He brought his dowsing twigs

and walked all round the garden in a mazy motion, pursued by Bob Gilbert who stuck in bamboos to mark subterranean channels. All part of a scheme to please English Heritage and attract maintenance and development grants. We also had Frank Hamel-Cooke to stay while he painted the overmantel in pastel colours.

On Sunday evening I took Jemima and a friend to give Higgy some daffodils. We had to wake him up and he stared rather uneasily, looking blotchy but happy to talk. The nurses said he'd been raiding the fridge so they have had to hide food from him. Apparently he gobbles up leftovers, but Sally Ann, the matron, says she is not worried because his weight stays the same. I didn't have much success with conversation, mainly about Mima's school, but then it was my fault for coming so late.

Mima was a bit shocked that his room was so small and he didn't have enough things of his own, and I tried to explain that quite apart from the cost he didn't notice that kind of thing and would not understand if we moved him. But she does have a point, and I will ask the sister to look out for a larger room.

Sunday 3rd May

One of those wonderful sunny days in May when I wished the garden was open for its own benefit – but it's the NGS (National Gardens Scheme) weekend and we are only allowed expenses. We sat on the stone steps with coffee, watching the ginger cat startle two elegant cock pheasants – neither party very confident. Caro collects another headless mouse for the deep freeze for the Prysor–Jones pet fox, who is claiming the whole bag today.

We walked around the garden thinking of all those things to be done. I must go down and sweep chipped paving and dust which gives the whole place a derelict look; it's an endless task unless you only look in one direction at a time. Yesterday we took quite a lot of thistles out of the warm border above the pools, and it looks fine if you ignore the ground elder and shepherd's purse.

Mima and I called in at Fritham again on the way to London on Easter Monday. His room looked untidy and old letters and Christmas cards were lying in the window-sill. Obviously he no longer has any sense of objects around him, and the daffodils we brought seemed of only momentary value. We took him for a short walk in the sun over the cattle grid which he negotiated expertly; we were both for some reason concerned that he would read the 'Nursing Home' sign and discover the truth about his 'holiday', but the thought now seems quite out of place.

Saturday 24th May

Friday was my father's 86th birthday and I had the enjoyment of taking to see him Gilbert Longden, who has just celebrated his 90th and has all his wits about him, unlike even some of our generation. Higgy was not in a state to receive anyone when we arrived and I had some mopping up to do in his bathroom. However, I got him along to the library where Caro and Gilbert were waiting. On the way he mumbled the splendid sentence, 'I've got the whole passage in my interest' – perhaps meaning he found the nurses friendly – but still sounding as though he was the 4th Earl walking through the parliamentary lobby or the huts in Chatham Dockyard.

He spotted the boxes of Ferrero Rochet chocolates Gilbert had brought and we poured out small glasses of sherry and opened some birthday cards. We had some gentle chat and I tried to steer him into the garden but we soon came back through another door and I thought he'd had enough. We said goodbye and left him waiting for lunch, but a few minutes later matron called us along as he had fainted. It was all too much, probably the combination of our visit, the heat and his insistence on wearing heavy clothes.

He was trundled dramatically along the passage and soon recovered lying on his bed, but looked very grey. We had to leave, but I rang back later and by then he'd already been back with the nurses, tucking into birthday cake.

Friday 3rd July

He was lying, half dozing, in his room when Rob and I came in today – the first visit we have made together. He didn't recognise either of us. I drew the curtains back and asked if he knew who it was and he parried, 'Someone who is going to let all the light in.' However, we were told that 'they' (he) would be pleased to welcome us in. So far, so good.

One of us asked, 'Do you know where you are?' He said he thought he was in a hotel in France and had been there about a week. He mentioned Mapperton as a place he would like to invite people down to. We got him into a half upright position and he struggled to sign a birthday card for Betts who is 75 tomorrow. He looked through Rob's catalogue of garden pots and when I described Rob's new factory and foreign travels, he obviously felt some admiration for him.

Saturday 11th July

I dropped into the newsagents in Beaminster to ask if they could now change the 'V' Montagu to a 'J' on the morning paper. I suspected them, quite unfairly, of a hankering loyalty. 'He doesn't read them any more,' I explained, not wanting to admit he wasn't even there. They probably know anyway. Meanwhile the letter-box still says 'VR', but that's different.

Today is the day of the 'Asterix party', when 450 people will sit down to eat wild boar in a marquee. Mad, of course. There are Roman columns on the lawn, statues down the steps and menhirs beside the Orangery. People are teeming all over the Italian garden which has a wonderful atmosphere under PVC, even in a drizzle. Tony, Raymond and Roy Copp, three young American cousins, and masses of friends of the boys are helping. Mima is doing labels, Orlando is wandering round pursuing signs and a piano, followed by Louis. Luke is doing a marvellous organising job and we can now at last conceive of our own retirement (in jest, of course, because we are managing all right – but only just).

[The weather thankfully improved later and the party went on till 8.45 am.]

Friday 28th August

I've been making extra notes in my diary to record more precisely some of the strange things my father says.

I 'took him out' today, very conscious of the reversed roles from my time at Summer Fields, almost expecting him to complain that I wasn't taking him anywhere nice enough. He was sitting happily as usual at the round table with all the other 'ducklings', waiting for bread, and was a bit disappointed that I was taking him away. 'Where are we going?' he kept saying as though I was a jailer; perhaps I was. But he enjoyed the outing: the sun was shining and it was a delicious, pastoral day driving past all the stray ponies and cows and bright purple heather in the New Forest.

We first went to The Bell Inn, near the golf course at Brook, and it was comfortable and so like Fritham House that he thought he was back where he started. We had a spot of trouble in the gents, but were soon happily sipping beer – he swapped my shandy for his stout – and eating halibut and paté starters. I talked to him about the family and Bill Guy's recent death and he seemed to take that in. I mentioned Copse Barn and Wytherston; he looked puzzled and said, 'I can't remember unless you tell me exactly where it is.' Then I told him at length about our Greek holiday and he said three times: 'Are you talking about the South of France or somewhere like that?'

After lunch we drove across some of the wilder roads towards Fordingbridge and he obviously enjoyed it but asked anxiously, 'Do we end up with something we know?' We got as far as Deadman's Hill – a lay-by at the junction of two bleak valleys – and he said firmly, 'I think we ought to turn back.'

When we eventually got back to Fritham House he was confused and said, 'There isn't anything very much for us here' and then said enigmatically: 'It's very like the hotel where you and I are.' I felt a bit trapped as I realised that in his mind he was still on the way to somewhere else ('home'?) and was depending on me to get him there – not for the first time. Luckily one of the young men rescued me; he came along the passage cheerfully and said 'Like a coffee, Monty? Biscuit? I'll bring it along to your room'; and, suddenly, he *was* at home – and I was away again. Before I left him in room 14 he said, 'Come and see me whenever you like.'

Monday 12th October

I went in again briefly on October 2nd, taking my niece Caterina. I remember Caroline was moody and went for a drive in the forest. He was in his room watching TV and polite, although not especially interested in us. Shirley and Joyce went a few days later, taking his remade corduroys, and reported that he was well but seemed to have forgotten Mapperton.

I was thinking of him again today because I have come down for a week and have to confront the question: 'Do I live here now, or do I still feel he is living here?' It's not that he's a ghost but... well, his spirit is here all right, and I am still rejecting it. If he lives another five years or more, am I going to find it harder to adjust as I get older?

It was the turn of the garden today. Our friend Georgina Eyre (Gorg) has been here giving advice on the English Heritage replanting scheme and walking about with Caroline and a stonemason. Of course we need the grants for maintenance, but I cannot help thinking once or twice that I am just helping 'him' – even if he has forgotten the place. I know these thoughts are wrong.

Gorg has asked Bob Gilbert for details of garden levels and so Bob has recruited me as surveyor's assistant. A bit like the clapper boy in a film called *The Draughtsman's Contract*, I have to stand with the two metre stick at strategic points while he lines up his levels on a tripod. I'm quite enjoying it as it enables me to see details of the garden and what needs doing while I'm standing shivering. It's surprising how often the ground falls two or three feet when you think you are level with it. I have also learned since the party in July how vast spaces can be filled or altered by human endeavour, purely for entertainment or aesthetics. A lot of that effort has been my father's, and I am, grudgingly, enjoying the results.

We need to collect all his photos of the garden which are bundled in a cupboard, especially those which tell us about the loss of tree cover. Some show the building of the Orangery, too. I went in there yesterday and found that the plants are coming on well with Kirsty's devotion – another thriving memorial of Victor Montagu's ghost. Or 'Poppa spooki', as we used to say as children, referring to 'my father's ghost' in the probably apocryphal Danish version of *Hamlet*.

Tuesday 10th November

8.15 a.m. is one of the best times of day, when you emerge from the stone doorway with a cup of coffee and drink in the freshness of morning – the sparkling sunlight in the valley garden, the sounds of dripping and thawing from yesterday's rain, the cries of the Jacob's sheep and the cockerels. How lucky we are, in spite of all the moans and groans which go with manorial life. That golden bantam cock is probably enjoying the last few days of life before the fox gets him – and I didn't mean that to be an allegory of my father! This morning he was chasing a hen pheasant past the wooden sculpture in the pool garden. Valerie Dalton saw Mr Fox in the drive two weeks ago; the hungry season approaches.

Rob and I went over to Fritham on October 30th and took our old bird out to lunch. We sat beside the open log fire in The Bell, chatting with a bit of effort. He had a good appetite but could hardly take in the information I brought him about a painting of the 3rd Countess of Sandwich that he had unfortunately sold for a song to Birmingham Art Gallery. I decided not to show him my new Save the Children book – restraint which was an achievement of its kind, because I have always tried to show him things I have done – still, it seems, the little boy needing encouragement.

Sunday 31st December

I took our friend Peter de Roos in to see him on Friday, and without knowing it Peter reinforced some of the sense of propriety and obligation I am supposed to have towards the old man, which certainly does need boosting. Peter used to telephone his mother every day for more than a year before she died.

We talked to him at his usual place at the round table – this time empty, as it was mid–morning. He was very taken by the Snoopy mug he was having his coffee in, and kept repeating the words on it. When we left he asked, rather unexpectedly in his old way, 'When am I going to see you again, Boysy?', which touched us both. Peter is also staying as a 'non–shooting' guest as we have a house full of guns this weekend and we are both very relieved to find someone prepared to talk about something else.

1993

Friday 22nd January

Caroline went to sleep in the car while I dropped into Fritham for half an hour. It was mid-afternoon but drizzling and I found him on his bed dozing. He was pleased to see me and sat up when someone brought us in a cup of tea. I was depressed to see that no one had tidied the window-sill: old Christmas cards lay about, the plants were gone and the Hilaire Belloc volume was damp. I tried to convince myself that all nursing homes are understandably overworked, but I think I will drop them a line.

I soon cheered us both up by reading him Belloc aloud and he guffawed when he recognized familiar lines from 'Matilda', 'Lord Lundy' and many others, known to most politicians and repeated endlessly at home when we were all younger. We talked as usual about Mum and where she lives, and about who is coming to see him – and who is not, in spite of a reminder letter I sent round at Christmas to describe where he was; a good idea of Kate's and obviously appreciated by friends.

'I do still have a house, do I?', was one of the more awkward ones which makes me wonder again if there is any point in moving him nearer home. But there really isn't.

Saturday 30th January

Les Way died suddenly in his sleep on Saturday night after winning a tin of rice pudding in a pub at Broadoak. He was only 53. He worked on the estate for 26 years and I got on well with him in spite of various differences. My father was very close – rather too close – to his family. Yesterday we had the funeral in Beaminster and Ethel kindly put out her hand to me on the way out of the service. I realised this was really for my father and afterwards I dropped in some white carnations from all of us, with his name clearly on the label.

The drizzle goes on relentlessly, and I wish I were in India like Jemima, John Major and the England cricket team. Andrée and I looked out of the office window at a white deer climbing up the wood behind the garden, so there are compensations!

Sunday 7th March

On Friday afternoon I gave him a long drive through the New Forest to Beaulieu, pausing at the gate but he needed reminding that Lord Montagu – 'your cousin' – lived there. We backed into a ride further on, ignoring a notice saying 'Beaulieu Estate – Private' so that he could have a pee. An estate worker drove past and stared at us, and I got ready to put our case, but he went on. 'Anyhow we've got every right to be here,' I said, and my father smilingly agreed. Years ago, he might have been shooting in that very wood.

He kept asking if we were on the way back. I pointed out views of the forest and played the King's College recording of the psalms so as to focus his mind a little, replaying 'Let the people praise thee, O Lord' from Psalm 67, the psalm read in Parliament which he was always fond of. I talked to him about Mapperton, but he wasn't clear about it. I asked him if he could remember his father's Christian name, and touchingly he said he couldn't, but ought to be able to.

Back at Fritham, we had tea in his room and then he seemed to want to show me something and walked round the corridor of the converted 'stable' and back. I sat with him in the day room and chatted to some of the others who were staring at me and pointing, 'Isn't he tall?' I was longing to leave but he had one last, confused try: there were some other rooms I could see if I liked, and I could stay, and have breakfast in the morning. This bit was testing: he always liked his breakfast, and knew that I did. But soon I was back in the car and away.

Thursday 18th March

The heron trick has failed. Perhaps my father was right – he used to use an owl. Goldfish and frogs have been disappearing rapidly from the garden pools, and Groves, the garden supplier, have given us a plastic heron to deter the real one, which arrives every morning looking fatter and unperturbed. They told Shirley herons were more territorial than owls.

Last night Alex Caccia and I propped it up on a stake beside the lower pool, on the spot where the heron peers into the water. I came down at 7.45 this morning and went straight out to see. There as usual, this time actually sitting on the pond, was the heron which immediately flew off down the valley, flapping its huge wings until it settled on a bank, waiting for a better moment. Kirsty and Tony and I stared after it. Perhaps he thought it was his mate, said Tony. Later Kate and I went out and the heron circled aggressively over us and croaked at the plastic mate. Tony and Luke want to shoot it. I'll have to go back to Groves and get an owl instead.

Luke has finally got the wild boar. He came into the sitting-room on Tuesday evening, rifle slung over his shoulder and a pleased smile. We had Carrie Carey staying, who we hope is going to rent the Old Rectory. Basically the story is that the boar got out of Gray's Farm and wandered around Wytherston Marsh: Orlando had a go at it one night and found Nigel and others shooting pigeons, which didn't make him too pleased. The owner tried to feed it in the wood, but that didn't work. Luke then went out with George and found it near the larches. He shot twice, the second time as it was galloping past, and finished it off with a third. The owner promises to send over some, in true Asterix style.

Yesterday we had two men planting trees all around us, filling in holes in the avenues and on the bank opposite the garden where Timmy and I had put stakes in last Saturday while Georgina and Caroline stood on the lawn. It's quite a difficult job, especially communicating: Prince Albert apparently waved semaphores standing on the balcony at Osborne. They are mainly eight foot oaks and beeches and now look quite impressive.

Kate and Nicky are spending the night, and last night we had a little too much to drink chatting, speaking for myself, until I literally fell asleep on the sofa in mid conversation. I find with them that we are thinking of new subjects so fast that there is no time to finish any conversations.

Thursday 15th April

Luke and I dropped into Fritham on Easter Monday with a bouquet of church flowers – to my surprise, it is the first time Luke has been there for 18 months. I remember enjoying visits to my grandfather's 'Cottage'; I think he got something out of them too. But Higgy is different.

We fished him out of the day room into the 'library', with its plastic sofa and lines of artificial book cover shelving. Still, it vaguely evokes the library at home. He asked as usual where we were and we had this extraordinary sense of timelessness, unable to fix him in France or the New Forest. I had to remind him how kind the staff were and how well he was looked after, to prevent him wandering into feelings of homelessness. However, he said once that he wanted to go home, as he had on the telephone on Sunday.

'Dad is 50 years old,' said Luke brightly: 'Your son.' The old face peered at me and beamed, 'That's very good.' I added that Mum was over here staying with Kate, but he only flickered. There were too many strands in the information, and I am only slowly learning how to spin one at a time.

When we got up to go, there was an unforgettable sight, like a human sculpture: two stooping men came slowly out of the dayroom just in front of us, with my father falling in behind. They followed each other like fairground cars down the passage, all three moving curiously in formation.

Luke said afterwards that he thought Higgy had deteriorated a bit, but was still his recognisable self. I'm too close to notice any change.

Monday 3rd May

I dropped into Fritham late in the evening with Louis, tired after two National Gardens Scheme days which raised over £600 plus house tours. I gave Louis a walk near the iron grid, and we trod gingerly over it to find the grass.

My father was lying down but quite happy to chat. I brought him apple juice and an apple twig in flower from the tree opposite the dovecote at Mapperton. At one point he sat up sharply and looked round and asked: 'Where am I exactly?' I must remember to bring Cyril Reason's picture of the ponds for him to look at.

These diary entries are now almost like remembering someone in your prayers, when you feel slightly guilty, the prayers are not long enough. There is not much to record, but the discipline of recording is still a valuable exercise and creates a time when I can quietly remember him. Otherwise time and hectic life will completely overtake him and he will be nothing more than a fortnightly Midland Bank cheque. The bill, incidentally, has gone up: when I showed some surprise, they said it was because of his incontinence.

Saturday 22nd May

We had 75 Historic Houses Association (Wessex Branch) members and friends to dinner and spent most of the day preparing for it, with drizzle setting in. For this reason I couldn't go over to celebrate my father's birthday – instead Kate and Julia took him out to lunch and found him OK. Kate stayed for the birthday cake – apparently the residents complained they preferred biscuits. By arrangement I rang him up after breakfast. He picked up the phone himself but didn't know who I was at first. Then he asked if I could drop in on the way, 'sideways', which I think meant 'if I happened to be passing'!

Tuesday 1st June

On Sunday I went over to Fritham to meet a couple from San Diego called Faulconer who had met Higgy way back in 1948, when he was sent over to thank US airmen for their war effort. They arrived at Mapperton instead, and simultaneously, so we never met, but I chatted to my father for half an hour. He was very verbose and jabbered fervently about nothing: I felt sorry to think there was so much energy to put to use. I offered him a delicious Saudi date wrapped in cellophane, brought back by C a week ago, but he evidently (perhaps going back to Siemens in 1927) thought of it as an electrode, prodded and pointed at it suspiciously, and said it needed a wire through the centre. We talked about Mum's photograph and he suddenly remembered she was 'very important' and knew she was important. As usual I explained where he was, and that I was going to Dorset, etc, and he suddenly darted the question: 'So where do I live?' and I had to say here and at Mapperton. Before leaving I recited 'Jabberwocky' to him, which he enjoyed, but it saddened me. Last night at 7 p.m. Orlando was ready to leave for London and I casually said, 'Sometime we must go to the Three Horseshoes in Powerstock', and he said, 'Shall we walk over there now?' Minutes later, with Louis and a 12-bore, we were striding up and down hills and nearly losing ourselves in valleys beyond Poorton. Lando picked an armful of wild yellow irises for Mum on the way but we both funked carrying them into the pub. He drove into Battersea after midnight, and during the night a joy-rider stole Luke's car and abandoned it.

Sunday 13th June

I took Perceval to see my father on the way down on Friday. We collected him from the day room as he was about to have lunch and the two old gentlemen nodded to each other, without much exchange. He did recognize P, I think, just before I said his name. 'Poor old man,' said P afterwards. Saturday started early with Shirley coming into our room to say Alfie'd had a stroke. We went up to find him still on the floor but comfortable, with Keith attending, and Joyce in control but staying in the kitchen. The ambulance arrived, then Dr Henstridge (?) from Maiden Newton, and off he went. We later heard he was better but would stay a night or two in Yeovil. I took Rosaleen and Sudhir Mulji around the garden and then up to see 'Coltleighville' – my name for the new shanty town at Coltleigh for rearing and releasing day-old pheasant chicks. Orlando described his plans to resurrect Hooke Court as a business centre, which have a high priority for him and C, although I am cautious. C discovered P hadn't written his address for the sermon at a wedding he was taking at West Coker that afternoon, so she quickly produced something for him on her word processor. We over-prepared for a visit by a party of 30 from the Georgian Group, giving them extra time to see round the house. Rosaleen and Sudhir joined in, rather amused by it all, even when Sudhir was discovered putting on socks in his room during the tour. Rain held off and we went up for tea, while P and C and S went to the wedding. In the evening the Markings came to supper. The following day we were 12 to lunch. And so on....

Tuesday 10th August

I went into Fritham on Sunday night on my way to London and as usual slipped in the back door, peeping to the left through his curtains which were drawn. No one was in sight, and I crept in to find a familiar snoring figure who suddenly stared at me. 'Hello,' he said, and then, 'boy—so', which brought relief. 'I've brought you a pot plant – from Mapperton'.

'Where?' he said. 'Mapperton.' It was a very blurred concept. 'Where is that?' Then when I described it, a string of disjointed sentences: 'That's my home, isn't it?' – 'Why am I here exactly?' – 'Where is this place?' I produced the usual platitudes and euphemisms about hotels and his doctor's recommendation. He nodded sadly that if he needed treatment he must stay there. We had some quite comical conversation during the hour I was there. I talked about Hinchingbrooke and showing people round and he said it was quite an effort. He remembered distinctly that his father lived in 'the Cottage' – this was up to 1962 when he died – and asked me if he was still living there now. I brought him the Goldsmiths' company magazine to read and when I said he was still a member he said: 'But I don't have any gold – at all!' At those moments we look at each other and relax and have a good guffaw, and it's difficult to remember what an ogre he could be. I gathered from the new matron that they had stopped the Daily Telegraph. 'He's not reading it. But he still pinches other people's!' she smiled. 'He's lovely.'

Tuesday 5th October

I rang up a few days ago to say I was coming in, and asked after him, and the matron said he'd just been past the office and beamed at them saying, 'Congratulations to you all!' I took in new clothes sewn with nametapes by Shirley, and a plant. I found him rather frail, staggering along the passage on the arm of two nurses, and very incontinent and quiet while I was there. He didn't want to go out and asked me to shut the window which I'd just opened, murmuring that I was 'better dressed' than he was. When he saw the clothes he said: 'I don't know whether I've got enough to put them safely in a ship or train.'

He then said abruptly that he wanted to go home, but his sentences tailed off: 'I'm not quite feeling that this place is not...'

I made reassuring noises and he said: 'They tell me it's very comfortable so that's what I...' (did he mean, ...have to accept?) We watched the Tory conference at Blackpool on TV and I tried to point out Heath and Robert Cranborne and he said very brightly, 'Isn't he an earl?' Then I read some Belloc and he seemed to appreciate Lord Lundy especially. He pointed to the book and asked 'Did I do this?' and then, 'It's done by you, isn't it?' I wished I could have told him I was Hilaire himself.

1994

Monday 24th January

5 p.m. – suppertime at Fritham. He was eating most of the time I was there, sitting beside the bed. Pasta, spinach and potato were being speared in turn like fish. Mumble mumble... 'It's very good'... rhubarb... mumble. 'I shall stop now;' but then goes on. After a few minutes I asked him who I was and he smiled and said, 'You're my brother,' which I took as a great compliment. I only felt sad later when telling the story to others. Then jelly and cream and pears, shovelled away like fuel into a hungry furnace. He pauses, toying with a pear on his spoon: 'I don't think I'll go on speculating its [the pear's] meaning, I think I'll give it up.' Pity he couldn't have said the same about the Anti-Common Market campaign. He seemed recharged, and conversation suddenly picked up. I told him some of our struggles while moving Orlando into his house in Fulham. 'I expect he's a very hearty boy,' he said. Not far off the mark. He's gone off with his brother to chase whales in the Caribbean, literally but from the air, in cousin Dru's plane.

Then he darted a look at me. 'Where are we actually?' I told him and he said, 'Well, we've had a very nice time,' which probably referred to the jelly. I asked him warmly: 'How are you, are you keeping well?'

'Just,' he replied, in a long-suffering tone I had known for years. This was the week we had the four lead fountains stolen from the Italian garden, right under our noses. They'll be in Bristol or Amsterdam by now [they were actually recovered in Putney a year later].

Tuesday 8th February

On arrival at Fritham I had this extraordinary sense first of emptiness without him and then his massive presence, almost larger than life. He was 'watching' the 6 o'clock TV news in his room when I came in. I returned him a panoramic photograph of Dorset fields I had taken, which he seemed to like. I then showed him a letter to him from the working man's club in Huntingdon of which he is still president and he said, 'You take it.' I was about to leave when he seemed to want to show me something, and got heavily up. He had difficulty with his stick. He perhaps wanted to take me to the day room but then indicated he wanted to go 'upstairs' – presumably to bed, in an earlier incarnation. The male staff had already warned me he needed two or three to support him in the corridor – he was 'slowing up' and had had one or two falls. A few steps outside the door and I managed to steer him round, back to his room, where I left him to the nurses.

Thursday 3rd March

He was sitting apart in the day room, looking hot, wearing a short-sleeved jersey under his jacket in bright sun, obviously dozing after lunch. 'When do you have your rest?' I asked, to remind him of his nursery and get a reaction. (Why does the younger generation always want a reaction?) I felt he was irritated by the question so I offered him a choc ice and he ate half of it, after some hesitation, and felt refreshed. I got him up for a walk and it was such an effort that he sat down again immediately. Then his turn came for an eye test in the 'library' across the corridor. The young nurse was expecting a lot, keeping professional standards, and she saw me frown at some of her questions. He was long-suffering and groaned a bit, but then read the third line of letters quite well and endured the pupil-searing torch. Then we slowly walked back to his room and C held his hand just before leaving. She said she could have stayed another hour holding it; it was one of the few ways of getting a message through.

Thursday 5th May

I told him about the Channel Tunnel opening today and he said, 'Are they doing it?', seeming to comprehend. I told him the Queen would be going through it. 'She may be rather bored, if not frightened,' he said. I told him he was going to be 88. '88?' he asked incredulously. 'Older than your father,' I said but got no reaction. 'How old was your grandfather when he died? When was he born?' I tried, but got only the hilarious rhyme 'You're going to mend his lawn?' so I gave up. [In the end he outlived his father by only a few weeks.]

Saturday 21st May

A film company is coming down to make a film called *Restoration* with top stars in the garden, and is bringing its own moonlight – a 115-foot arc lamp on a crane. The cockerels have got to be cooped up to reduce the dawn chorus, but I can't think how they will stifle Westland helicopters. Meanwhile 15 lambs have been born to Kate's healthy Jacob's ewes; one was still-born and another immediately covered in hail but now healthy. The pheasants' eggs are turning up at a terrific rate. Deer are happily multiplying. My father is 88 tomorrow and we are dropping in for tea.

Monday 18th July

I came downstairs a bit jaded this morning – the morning after Brazil won the World Cup and the weekend the children had all been staying for Tamsin Hichens' wedding in Sherborne. I was carrying a bundle of yesterday's newspapers through the house and suddenly remembered my father doing exactly the same. Perhaps I am copying him without realising it, in all kinds of hidden ways. I sometimes think of him during house tours, which he used to do at Hinchingbrooke. One memorable moment last week was seeing a queue of eleven ladies from Basingstoke outside our one (public) loo. I had to let half the queue into the house. On Saturday we missed the lobster at the wedding because we had to get back for the Torquay Horticultural Society. They were standing patiently outside in the heat, and C kindly poured 27 glasses of water for them. During the tour I was describing the problem of gardens and I actually said, 'Aren't we all having a terrible time keeping them up,' meaning the extra weeding and watering this summer. I was finally including myself with the gardeners – including my father? Just because I have been watering four pots and strimming and weeding a yew hedge.

We are going to see him today. A fortnight ago he was wrapped in blankets on a hot day, and he was refusing to wear shoes and I thought we were nearing the end, but then heard he was up and into the garden. Kate couldn't get much response last week. I wish we could give him a brighter end to life with more to look at; but would it be for our own benefit? He seemed in good heart, and wanted to come out. I drove him to a clearing in the forest and we ate ice creams – or one–third in his case, the rest finished by the dog. I asked him if he was feeling well and he replied looking at the view that he was 'very interested in it all'. I told him I was going to London – 'I'd gladly come with you'. Back at Fritham we were followed into the day room by a rather beautiful elderly woman who came very close to him and he smiled at her. Then she touched his forehead and I winced, saying I would have to be off. 'I'm coming with you,' he said immediately – it was a hilarious moment – and we all three started a slow procession back to his room until a nurse managed to steer her off.

Monday 25th July

I walked through the wood with Louis to see if the rides had been cleared of debris after felling. A pair of buzzards flew out – probably the ones which had nested in a Douglas fir and were rescued by Michael, the keeper. Some deer were chased out of the field up to me by a tractor, most likely Jeffrey Fooks who has been topping the lower field. The scenes of destruction had improved since I complained and the rides were clear – but I forgot to check if they'd replaced the fence. Further up I suddenly saw a thousand tiny heads bobbing, some even trying to fly out of the pen.   I came back past Keeper's Cottage, its bright garden hidden behind a straggling hedge, past the new plantation which is coming up well, and met Lal and her shy blonde son Ed, pushing a wheelbarrow which she said she uses to put the dustbin out. We chatted about the fancy dress she is organizing at the fair next month, and she asked if I had smelled the limes in the drive. No, but I must. On such warm evenings the hassle of estate management (which frequently makes us wonder if it's really worth it) melts away.

Wednesday 17th August

It's always disappointing when one of your closest friends misunderstands you – even when he's a dog. When I said, 'Good dog, good Louis', I meant, what a very good companion you were on that long trek up round the woods above Loscombe; but as I was clearing away the supper, as usual he thought I was talking about more food. But I also had to thank him for not disappearing into the pheasant pens or getting soaked in muddy streams and keeping to heel when asked, even towing me up steep banks through thick bracken as we negotiated the 'new' lost wood, the Mythe Willow Beds, behind the fields of Mapperton Farm which we bought last year. I also had to check part of the new track from Mythe to Burcombe where over-enthusiasm on the part of both the shoot and farmers has led to riders' protests. The yellow stone laid will mean a better track for all users in the end, but at the moment it looks like the Golden Road to Samarkand and a lot of rolling and raining and grass growing will be needed before the riders are satisfied. I have been placed in a tricky position with the Council who should have been informed and have quite rightly sent their rights of way officer up with an engineer to see that we are doing it properly. If 'we' is the right word: I often have the feeling that owners are simply holding the line between interested parties and cannot afford the luxury of a 'personal view'. This morning I took West Country Cleaning up to quote on hosing out the two reservoirs. The leaner man, the one who has to climb through the hatch into the mud and has a special certificate, turns out to be John Colfox's gamekeeper: I'm not sure which job is the disguise, but it easily took me in. Mum is over from France and stayed last weekend which was a great treat. Kate came to lunch today to drive her back to Wiltshire where they will gorge on Bembridge prawns. After some hesitation I have cleared out all my father's old handmade Lobb shoes and have found two pairs of usable slippers. Kate is next due to go to Fritham and will take them in. I rang this evening and the sister says he has been out in the sun but has refused to join the outing to Bournemouth – which shows he is in splendid form.

Tuesday 11th October

At Fritham today we went out on the verandah, then pottered courageously into the garden where he had a pee against the back of a hedge. Well, why not: it's an effort to get anywhere in a hurry. But he is heavy to support, and smelly. Luckily he pointed with his stick at the sun, and we ambled back to the white plastic chairs. Conversation with him is about 150% effort for 25% return – about the same as an old steam engine. I gave him a booklet on Hinchingbrooke, with familiar images of gables and roofs. He paused on the Buck print. I showed him the front entrance and asked if he remembered Mr Small, the butler. 'He was very kind and helpful,' he said. I asked him what message I should take to Julia (who is very fond of him). 'Who?' 'Your daughter.' All he said was, 'I'm not doing anything' — which had some logic. Then he said, with old cunning: 'What do you think I should say?' (i.e. now that you've heard me give a non-answer). I lost patience. 'Tell her you want to go to the Party Conference in Bournemouth.'

Monday 31st October

Monsoon at Mapperton — 4 inches in about 36 hours, and water is pouring down from every direction. None of the trenches dug up on the road seem to have channelled it off. The man from General Accident of course arrived as I was up the drive clearing leaves from the endlessly blocked ditch above the Old Rectory. 'My husband's down the drain,' said Caroline cheerfully. The trouble is, it's too true. Every week brings a torrent of new work and new bills to follow, while our London income fades. We're living on the last of C's Middle East income, and I've hardly enough productive work. The children are still blissfully unaware and going on drawing on us — what choice do they have? Kate went to see Higgy and he was conspiratorial with her: why don't we leave by that door over there? Julia suggests she could bring him over here for tea — a good theory, but oh dear no. My father reminds me of George Foreman who aged 45 has sensationally knocked out his opponent: it was his son who passed out and had to be carried off.

Sunday 13th November

The rain and mist has been incessant, with leaves cluttering the drive and paths, blocking drains and gutters. Yesterday started typically with Orlando calling out, 'Leak in muniment room' as he rushed off to a smart shoot, so I went to mop up under a window and returned to find the cats finishing my breakfast on the kitchen table. Later on the Fooks' cows got out and David Puzey and I herded them off the road, but not before they had trampled all over the courtyard lawn. It's Armistice Sunday and I am about to dial Higgy in Fritham to remind him. Some hope. I got straight through and said, 'It's John, your son' and he began stuttering, 'I don't know where he is, I'm not at my desk...' and so I simply told him what day it was and to watch the TV and think of Drogo, and he listened obediently and said 'Right'. It's all pretty pointless but it colours the day – my day, more like. I found myself warmly thanking the male nurse who had brought him to the phone. I don't even know him – could it be that I now actually care more about him than Higgy? Yesterday I opened the side door of the outside loos, which has become a routine while there are shooting lunches in the Orangery. For security I usually remove all the framed photographs, but I hesitated and only took in the Hinchingbrooke group with King Edward VII and Grandpa, leaving the two Vicky cartoons of 'Hinch'. Well, why not, the shooting fraternity will enjoy them.

1995

Saturday 8th January

LETTER TO MY MOTHER

The light is suddenly coming up in the west, behind the stables, as the day's drizzle drifts away eastwards. I have just put away the garden tractor, pulling the heavy doors of the sawmill satisfactorily together and securing the huge Chubb padlock. Yesterday we pruned one of the vines in the orangery and so I was collecting the debris just inside the two blue gates — the ones which originally came from the kitchen garden at Hinchingbrooke. This reminds me that since the garden fountains were stolen a year ago we've bolted them back but have still done nothing to protect that side of the garden from marauders. At least the gates should be padlocked — one more key for the shoot and everyone else using the orangery — and perhaps we should find a new gate on to the drive. Oh well, I think I can write a convincing letter of intention to the new insurance company — who, incidentally, not only want us to rebuild the bridge over the stream (we are) but also to put up a lifebelt with signs over the pool saying 'deep'! (We did.)

We've just about cleared the bottles, burned the holly and other Christmas debris, and desks are piled with paper but I feel a little more buoyant, now that we can look forward a few weeks to the spring.

Snowdrops are coming out and we've spent some of today collecting fallen sticks among peeping daffodil shoots and inevitably treading on some. Also I have got work this month in the Christian Aid press office – fairly routine but I go back on the train this evening and start early on Monday which is good for the soul. Tomorrow Gemma and Mima and I are going to the Royal Court to see a new play about Rochester, and I'll drop in on Betts (who is much better although not going out much these days).

Caro is clearing up dresses and costumes in the attic after laying them all out for an expert who got very excited about the 18th century ones including the material used in chasubles. She's also making tea for her parents, having given P a corking Sunday lunch for which he came up specially. I must go and join them. C has a lot on because of stories arising from her Saudi visit before Christmas, plus estate and all the chores connected with her parents. And Orlando's about to arrive with a friend for a shoot.

Timmy, Martin Best and his son Theodore all sang brilliantly in the carol service on Sunday, making up for the loss of the brass band. We had Norah (King) and the Hobhouses for one meal, and a lot of 25-year-olds for New Year, and never seemed to have fewer than 20 – although Christmas Day was quiet with just the Haymans and Billy. Edward Montagu came one day – his mother's about to be 100 and the boys say she's got lots of good stories. Luke has gone off to Kenya with Adam but is back for Orlando's birthday and more shooting.

We heard your Christmas went well and you only had a row on the last day! Hope most of it was fun and that you enjoyed it. Cate seems to be a bit perkier and taking more interest in life.

Monday 6th February

Caroline and I spent an hour pruning apple trees in the orchard behind the tennis court. I of course thought a lot about the time my father spent here.

Thursday 16th March

'I've brought some daffodils for you,' I said loudly, trying to fill the silence. He lay there with his eyes firmly closed. But I hear he's still quite aggressive. He's just been 'turned' and the young nurse and I were cursed for tucking in a dangling leg. I am now sitting next to a red-faced figure of nearly 90 years, holding his trembling hands and thinking how much energy there has been in one life. His hands relax and I can sit back. One huge deep breath – then nothing – and I still wonder if he's breathing for a moment. Then I said the 'Our Father' rather slowly, with emphasis on the last five words. He opened his eyes several times and at the end I said 'All right?' twice, and I swear he breathed 'Yes' – twice back. Then I said 'Lighten our Darkness...' but by then he seemed to have slipped into a deeper sleep. However, he is so canny that I half expected to hear a sudden challenge as I made these notes: 'Johnny what are you writing?' But this time it never came.

Tuesday 28th March

My father finally died on Saturday, 25th March, in the early hours. We had been with him a few hours earlier and knew it would be soon. Ever since, we have been in a whirl of phone calls and all the details of his funeral. I have been in tears for very short moments – the latest when Clifford Howe practised the Chopin prelude no 20 he always played, using the swell on the organ.

This afternoon, soon after 4, the undertakers brought him back to Mapperton. I got cross about it because C thought I should be properly dressed to meet him instead of in gardening clothes – especially as we had arranged for him to be in a smart suit and Old Etonian tie. She was quite right. Tony had trouble trying to toll the bell slowly – it wouldn't. Peter Steele, one of the younger clergy in the Team, kindly came and we lit candles and said some prayers as he was carried up the aisle to the choir. Afterwards we pulled back the purple shroud and there was a wax face set in a grimace – as Robert described it to Kate – as though he disapproved of something. He usually did. I've just been in to snuff out the candles and I completely forgot he was there – he was suddenly staring up at me. I got a terrible shock and drew back the shroud for the night.

My thoughts this week seem mostly about the future: apprehension about the future of my life, concern about the children arguing, and Mima's challenge about the necessity of changing our name. But from time to time someone comes and brings back memories.

Thursday 9th June

LETTER TO MY MOTHER

There is something faintly amusing – and desperate – about starting this letter when I am wrapping presents (including H of L chocs) and getting tea for Sylvia's 83rd birthday party, and two Cuban photographers are simultaneously waiting in the garden for C and me to pose with watering cans and shears. It's for a page of a US magazine called Town and Country and they want it without electricity – presumably to perpetuate the myth of olde Englande. One can imagine readers:

'Oh look at this picture, they're still hand-clipping yew bushes over there Gertrude – look it's the Earl and Countess of Sandwich, it's too cute.'

It's now six hours later, believe it or not, after little 'shoots' all over the garden and we have only just finished. Poor S and P got abandoned with a friend after we had had the cake and 'birthday shoot' on the lawn. Proper English tea, good as on the Thai Airways playing cards. One picture shows bejewelled Caroline like Venus in one of the alcoves in front of the house – I would pay money for that one. Sylvia will look good. But the whole thing was almost a fiasco and the pictures will no doubt end up like postage stamps. We haven't any idea which, if any, they will use and it doesn't come out till October so we'll try and forget all about it.

I have been enjoying the Lords but it takes time to appreciate. It's not too formal, and people are very courteous. I must have had since childhood the ability to walk cheerfully up to people and introduce myself, but I am

occasionally aware of being too friendly and as in any public school there
are examples of 'overstepping the line' — which can literally mean walking
over an extra piece of carpet (as Caroline found on entering the library
which is out of bounds to visitors). Jean Trumpington is always a great
relief because she doesn't have these terrible inhibitions. She also thinks I
need a bit of social push and has introduced me to people in the bar where
she is often found before lunch. I tend to visit the sandwich bar as I don't
like lunches and the barmaid said, 'Ooh' when she heard it was the Earl of
Sandwich and passed the news on to the next customer peer who thought
she was talking about a new variety.

I enjoy the secret route from Westminster tube through a turnstile and across Palace Yard and Westminster Hall. There's a shared desk but it's very nice to have a locker, notepaper and free inland phone calls and you can hide out in corners. I haven't yet made a speech or cracked the committee system and it may take months to do both. I am getting a lot of advice from a few other younger peers – not the .younger Tories, some of whom are of course largely 'stuffy' (my father's word) with the exception of Lord Cranborne. I am seeing Stormont (Chris) on Tuesday and will introduce him to Betts on the terrace. The day after Luke is coming in to meet Bishop Barrington Ward and talk about Hiroshima. I have been trying to find out about a missing aid worker in Chechnya. Monday I am lobbying Lady Chalker with a delegation from the aid agencies about Afghanistan. So I am slowly becoming active. I have joined the Commonwealth Parliamentary Association which means meeting annual curry lunches and possible invitations abroad. So it ain't a bad life, and I know there may be a time limit so am making the most of it.

Friday 16th June

This is only a brief postscript, because life has moved into a completely new phase. Poor Julia died last month and we are going to look after her 13-year-old Timothy. Tonight I spent an hour hacking away at a laurel up in the orchard, and was again suddenly reminded of my father outdoors. He was a good gardener, but I hardly remember him pruning or weeding – he much preferred mowing, driving the tractor, bonfiring, or cutting ivy and dead wood.

I thought of him yesterday, too, when I was invited for a drink by Roy Jenkins in the Lords where of course his contemporaries, who wished he had stayed there, have been very kind to me. I felt a little disloyal as I explained that my mother's political influence on me was stronger than his; however, I wasn't planning to join the Liberals immediately, if at all, and would remain on the cross benches (as I have). On the fence. Because, I said, I knew a lot of his friends and, in spite of everything, I believed in some of the things they did, and he had done. It's hard to explain.